The Deacon
and The
Wheel

Time Healed Me

Kenneth
McClain

For Mom, Myron, Greg, and Val

Contents

Foreward

All my life people have addressed me with one of the shorter derivatives of the name, Kenny, Ken or Kennay. My father, Lovie McDee McClain always, called me Kenneth. Occasionally, he would wonder aloud why I let people call me anything other than my given name. And I like my name. I used Kenneth when I wanted to be formal or when I believed it appeared more regal. At any rate, they say one of the sweetest things you can hear is your name. I agree.

I've heard it said that I have a cartoon face-a Saturday morning face. Maybe it's true, but maybe not. I do know that my face is my dad's face. However, before I go claiming to be his twin, I'm not. The twin distinction belongs to my brother, Myron. Nonetheless, my resemblance to my dad is un-mistakable.

My dad had a cheerful face, a fat face. It spoke to people in a happy, language. An inviting language. He was, as they say, easy on the eyes, and because he was, people were drawn to him. His personality, perfectly matched this appearance. He was receptive to people and he maintained a youthful image throughout most of his life. But around age 51, he got sick. His illness eventually took him, but before it dampened his otherwise youthful appearance. Dad lit every room. His voice was similar to James Earl Jones, filled any room, and his smile was a wide, full 32 teeth smile. He laughed from way down in his belly. He had fat brown cheeks, and a head full of hair. His face was unlined, despite age. I am frequently told I do not look my age. Many people tell me, "Kenny, you look younger than…." however old I am. I always say, "Thank you, my mom and dad did this." They gave me superior DNA. I just manage what they made.

My father left an indelible imprint on my life and the lives of my siblings. We each had a unique relationship with him. But while we loved him, and it's obvious whenever we reminisce about him, it's funny because we were also terrified of him. I will re-phrase that to say-us boys were. My sister, the youngest and the only girl, could do no wrong. However, in retrospect, dad would not harm a flea except to say, "Get off my plate of food." His big bad persona was put on just to scare us when Mom said we misbehaved and to let Mom know he had her back. When she wasn't around, dad was as soft as newly spun laundry.

That energy has remained with me, despite the passage of time. His influence was huge, although he lived to be just 58. I was 34 when he died. A massive heart attack took him from us. My Dad was a modest man. He lived a humble life -he worked, as far as I know he never drank alcohol, he went to church, and he was a husband, a father, a son, a brother, an uncle and a friend. We loved him and enjoyed his company because of cheerful countenance. His quick wit, smile, and laugher lit a room. He fell un-expectedly ill six years before his heart attack. Although his diagnosis required medical treatment for the remainder of his life, he kept a brave face. I never saw or heard him express fear in the face of challenging medical conditions. He continued to live to the fullest level possible.

The pain of loss is an awful thing to bear. A good friend shared a saying with me: "pain shared is half as bad, and joy shared is twice as good." It's simple, yet true. Losing my dad was very painful. Luckily, I had family and friends who rallied to my support. The passage of time healed a lot of my grieving; I am firmly aware of his departure, yet comforted by his presence in the form of positive energy, lessons, and DNA from the man I loved so much.

In the Beginning

As a very young kid, I delighted in looking at my parents' huge treasure trove of photos. There were hundreds of pictures. My parents kept them in a small suitcase stored in the back of my mother's closet. With permission I'd go into their bedroom go directly to where I knew the suitcase was, pull it from the back of the closet, and sit on their bedroom floor, going through the photos for hours. All the pictures told a story. Most of them were taken in black and white. There were a few in color, but those looked as if they had been taken in a studio.

There was one of my brother, Myron, and me. I could tell it was a studio photo; it was in color. I was around three and Myron one. I was all decked out in a suit and bowtie. I must admit, I was a sight to behold, dapper and handsome. I was clearly a boy, with a small face, a recent haircut, bright, curious brown eyes, and freckles, lots of freckles, dotting my nose and cheeks. Myron appeared ambiguous. He was cute, and alert, with his chocolate brown complexion, and with his hair braided, he could have easily been mistaken for a chubby baby girl instead of my little brother. There was another color studio photo in that collection, one of me and my cousin Morris. We were both dressed in our best suits and seated side by side. The photo might have been taken on Easter Sunday. We were impressive in our church clothes-our Sunday go to meeting clothes. Morris and I are 10 months apart in age.

Among the photos in the suitcase were dozens and dozens of photos of my parents from what looked like when they were dating and possibly just married. My mom was, and is a beautiful woman, and those early photos captured her radiance. I would look at the photos and think to myself, even at age eight or nine "Wow, my mom is a real stunner." In the photos my dad looked as if he had been struck by thunder. His expressions were all over the place from, "man I really am over my head with this beauty, to maybe I need to go out and play the lottery." You could tell he was over the moon with my mom. In each picture they looked happy and well matched as a couple. My mom was 5'7", which was tall for a woman in the early 1950's. She was definitely a slender rose and stood almost shoulder to shoulder with my dad, who was 5'9." Among color photos was one of my parents on their wedding day. It was classic.

The photos that always drew the most interest and curiosity from me were of my dad in the military during the Korean conflict. They were really good pictures, and there were lots that captured all kinds of daily military activities. In several he was young, in good physical shape, strong, and handsome. And although the photos were black and white, there was a hint of glamour to them. And a very strong presence. I got a sense of life in the military at that time through the pictures. Surprisingly, there were many white soldiers' arm in arm, side by side, laughing and talking with their black peers. Their shirts off, some needed a shave, or not and most were relaxing. These photos had to have been taken between1950 and 1952. How ironic that this treasure trove of photographs showed black and white soldiers, young men, just over the age limit for the military, yet-not old enough to legally drink in the U.S. Nevertheless, they were all military men, representing one United States of America. Those young men faced the realities of combat, which meant, in some instances, sacrificing life and limb abroad, while a world away in their home country, The United

States of America, Jim Crow laws, segregation, prejudices, and inequality were as common as every day of the week. These same guys might not have spoken to each other at home, and might have double down on that sentiment if they were from any state south of the Mason-Dixon Line. As I got older, looking back, I wondered if serving together changed any attitudes of those who harbored prejudices prior to serving in the military.

The photos were taken in the field (out in the open). I'm certain a lot were personal photos they shared with each other, and some were taken by a military photographer. In many of the photos, my dad reminded me of Sidney Poitier; strong, handsome, regal, and heroic. In the suitcase with the photos, there was a box. It was larger than a ring box and about the width of a post-card. Its depth was maybe 0.25", and an intricate design on the front, with a U.S. emblazoned stamp. I knew the box held something important to my dad. I opened it hundreds of times.

It held a Purple Heart he was awarded after he was wounded in combat. I knew of my dad's injury before I knew of the Purple Heart and what it meant to receive one. One day, my dad told me in great detail about the incident. It was a heartbreaking story of death, pain, and loss friends. He did move on from what he saw and experienced as a U.S. Marine but he never forgot. Although he told me that story, I did have questions about the military photos: who took them and why were they taken. Questions I never got around to asking, and to this day, I don't know why I did not ask.

Now dad is in Heaven; of this I am certain. I no longer mourn him the way I did when he first departed. But I do miss him still. I'm comforted in knowing his whereabouts and that he's with loved ones. One of my brothers is there, as are my grandparents, maternal and paternal; aunts and uncles; a few friends, but this book is about my dad. My heart is at peace regarding him.

He wasn't perfect, but he was everything my mom, brothers, sister, and I needed. And it was good being his child. He was funny, handsome, smart, and affirming. Of course, in retrospect, I say he was great. But I don't say he was great because he was my dad. I say he was great because he earned the moniker the old-fashioned way. He did the necessary things, in my eyes, to be thought of this way. I'm grown, and with a degree of certainty, I can distinguish various levels of achievement in myself and, on occasion, in others. My truth is, (and I hate to say it) that I'm not great. There, I said it! I wish I were. I wish I could stand before the man in the mirror, and smile, stare or glare even, and proclaim my greatness, but in all honesty, I cannot. I'm good on my best days, but okay most of the time. I do try.

My claim to fame is, and this is a fact, that on any given day, I can get my sister to laugh. That's it.

However, my dad, or rather, our dad, was great. He never gave up on a challenge. He showed grit when confronted with adversity, and he excelled in life where it mattered most-what your family feels for you and thinks of you not only when you're gone, but also when you're with them day in and day out. He taught us and provided for us. Every day, I enjoyed his company. He was never too busy, too tired, or too preoccupied to give me or my siblings his time if we asked for it. Oh, I am not saying that at times I did not grow tired of his parenting rants, or that I did not at one time believe myself to be smarter than my parents, or that we did not have our disagreements, as all parents and children do, but they were just moments, and I knew enough to not try to drag them on for days on end. What I'd give for just one of those moments today with my dad.

He parented us for 34 years, and he loved his family, wife, children, and grandchild. Stephanie, my eldest child, was the only grandchild he had at the time of his passing. He was humble, hardworking, devoted, and God-fearing, and his loved showed. More than anything else, the best gift my dad gave me was the ability to love as a father. I received this gift from watching him and from being his son. He wasn't an overly affectionate guy, a hugger or kisser, per se, but you knew he loved you. I did, and I also felt protected.

I love my kids more than I ever imagined I could. Parenthood, for me, is magical. Who knew! I have my very own fan club of people I helped make, who resemble me not only in some physical way but also in some mannerisms. My dad's presence as an everyday parent in my life taught me how to forego selfish endeavors so that I could attend to things basic and significant in the lives of my kids. I'm most like him in this way parenting. My own life's trials, victories, and defeats have been based on how I've chosen to navigate my life and God's daily blessings. Parents rarely, if ever, discuss with their children the sacrifices made on their behalf, but it becomes oh so clear to you, once you have children, that sacrifices must be made.

When Dad died suddenly and unexpectedly one morning from a massive heart attack, it was painful for us and for the countless others who knew and loved him. Losing Dad was a lesson for me on the fleeting status of our lives.

So, I stand in my dad's shadow. I stand there because I understand the morals of the man who raised me. Even though I'm taller in physical height than he was, I'm not as tall as him when I stand on my legacy (to date) compared to his. My dad had integrity, was slow to anger, abhorred gossip, was charitable, was my mom's rock, and was a proud African American man. He loved his in-laws and saw to it when I was young that we took regular cross country trips to visit my mom's family, who at that time lived in the Mid-west.

I've learned a lot in the wake of losing my him. I'm reminded to dot "i"s and cross the "t"s of the responsibilities that occupy my life. But, understanding the fragility of physical life, and how fleeting it can be, is also a reminder to live as fully as possible. In the haste of daily living, I'm reminded by his example to take time to give thanks to God for the day's blessings. In the spirit of a servant, I try to serve God every-day in my daily living. I honestly cannot tell you if I'm successful or failing in this capacity as a servant, but I do know every attempt I make to be what I believe God intended me to be makes me feel better about the totality of my life. I feel my dad's love for me every day. What I learned from him keeps me safe. I am reminded of his presence when I shave, brush my hair and teeth, and simply wash my face. Like I said, my face is his face. And although I've heard it said that when someone dies, it's easy to see and remember only the good, I hope that for the purposes of these recollections, I present the entirety of the man I called Dad.

My mom and dad were married for 36 years. My dad died two months short of their 37th wedding anniversary, two months short of his 59th birthday, and two months short of my 35th birthday. My mother never remarried.

As I get older, I wonder what my relationship with my dad would be today. I'm left with a longing for his companionship in real time. I have questions he could answer concerning parenting, marriage, work, activism, blackness, manhood, friends, family, finances, truthfulness, the government and more. Further, he would enjoy my asking him these questions. And a bonus of our relationship, for him, would be his grandchildren. My mom gets to enjoy them. I'm sure my dad would be tickled to death to see his grandsons and granddaughters, five in all + 1 step-grandchild.

I imagine everyone has a story to tell, but I never imagined the first story I'd choose to tell publicly would be this one, where I lay bare some facts of my life and my view of my father. My dad did not influence all areas of my life, thankfully. I would be embarrassed to think that my dad had anything to do with some of the ways in which I have lived my life, and I do not mean to suggest that he did. My forays into areas of difficult times, self-harm, and unimaginable and unthinkable dysfunction were of my own doing. I experienced teenage rebellion, adult transgressions, and curios excursions where and when I knew trouble existed. Those were all mine. Lovie, my dad, had nothing to do with those activities. His teachings and preaching's to us, (his kids), were all given with the intention that we'd learn and use that information to thrive at the highest levels possible. Because of this, we're good today and he would be happy to know it.

He started looking forward to our success when I was soon to be born. There is a form of socialization for men that's a rite of passage when a man becomes an expectant father. In the instant it becomes known that a baby is on the way, that man's brotherhood, consisting of the men in his life, (his family and friends), begin to muse about what it is like to have a son. All the conversation is about what (the potential son) will become and how his mannerisms will mimic those of his dad. He will be a reflection of the man's successful career. The conversations become all-encompassing as the baby's due date draws nearer. Men begin to foresee the destiny of the child. I have yet to meet a man who foresees the same for a daughter. It is only after the birth of a girl that a father can imagine a successful path for her, although it's highly likely that the girl can be more successful than her brother(s). This is just how the world works.

At any rate, men believe they will be manlier if they produce a son. It is a fallacy passed from man to man since the beginning of time. The reason, more than any other, is because of this socialization regarding becoming a dad. Every child after that initial boy can be a girl, but men's thoughts will go to having a boy first.

For my dad I was that son. The firstborn who came into the world shortly after my very young parents married. I imagine my dad was ecstatic-and my mom, too. I hope I have honored the name as they intended me to.

Mc Dee

I miss my dad. He's buried in my hometown, not far from the street where I grew up. I don't live in the town anymore, but when I did, I'd stop at the cemetery to visit his grave. I'd do this often mostly when I'd visit my mom.

Mountain View Cemetery is in Altadena, California just north of the city line of Pasadena. It sits just above the southern border street of Woodbury Avenue on North Fair Oaks Boulevard. It is directly across from Metropolitan Baptist Church. Everyone in Altadena, Pasadena, and the surrounding area knows of its location. Many of the deceased from the area are buried at Mountain View.

When I pull my car onto the cemetery's road, I'm immediately met by a huge oak tree that sits directly in the middle of the street. There is a small guard house adjacent to the tree, the mortuary offices are a stone's throw to the north. I see the tree as comforting, as if its sole purpose is to console visitors. I drive slowly past its outstretched limbs and branches. Entrance and exit lanes into and out of the cemetery are on either side of the tree. Once I'm past the tree and the guard house, I pull through big metal gates to enter the grounds, and I can usually make out the smell of freshly cut grass. Typically, somewhere in the distance, a groundskeeper is working. Sometimes I hear the engine of a seated mower. The groundskeepers do an excellent job tending the grounds. I have many friends and family who been laid to rest in the same cemetery: Rita Martin, my childhood friend, Debra McClain, my first cousin; Quentin Stepps, a childhood friend of my dad's and my godfather, and more. To see my dad, I make a slight right and head down the sloping road. I pass the resting place of Mr. Mills, a dear friend's father. After a minute, I turn gently to the left for another minute of driving, which then takes me to where my Dad rests. There is a rock and a concrete bin on the curb not far from his grave. I use the bin as a marker to know where he is, as well as a gravestone that has a small porcelain angel sitting on top. I walk towards my dad's grave, my eyes begin to mist, it's automatic. I start speaking to him not knowing if he hears me or not. When I visit him, my heart is always full. When I reach his resting place, I kneel and use my hands to sweep away any leaves and debris that have fallen over his name. I want to clearly see it on the face of his stone. Sometimes, I just sit there on the grass beside him. It's usually quiet and he's near a comfortable tree. But, if I'm in a hurry, I stand just in front of his gravestone and catch him up on the latest news about me and his grandkids, my children. I cry at that point; I can't help myself. I tell him the tears are because I miss him so much, and I ask him to hug my brother, Gerald for me, and in general give a shout out to those I know there with him. I try to make my visit neither too short nor too long, but I do spend the time I need to catch up. I don't have many opportunities to visit any more as I've been away.

The weather was beautiful that day of the funeral. It was coming upon early November in Altadena. The day was warm and sunny. I've long held the belief of late October to the end of November is the most beautiful time to see Pasadena and Altadena. It is a time when Santa Ana winds blow through San Gabriel Valley. The winds can be terrifying when they come, and it is not uncommon for parts of Altadena and Pasadena to be without power for hours or on occasion, a day or two. One year, my mother lost a pine tree and the overhead power lines behind her house. The winds toppled a tree that stood at least four stories and when the tree fell, it brought down the power lines with it. My mom and sister had to be evacuated to a hotel for three days. Nevertheless, when the winds come, they blow everything out, and we are left with a vision of perfection, which is the San Gabriel Mountains. The view seems endless. Leaves on trees bright orange as fall arrives late and the weather continues to stay above 65 F.

That day my wife, our daughter, and I took a short car ride from our home to my mom's house. A small gathering of mostly family was already there, including a few friends and neighbors. Everyone was milling about, going in and out of the house. A few core family members were waiting on cars that which would be sent from the funeral home to transport us to the chapel where the funeral was to take place. After entering my mom's house, speaking with her, and saying hello to those who had gathered, I went into the kitchen where I found my siblings, Myron, Greg, and Val. We enjoyed each other's company without saying much. Everyone was dressed in black. I remember standing at the kitchen sink, my siblings sitting at the kitchen table. I offered a thought; I said, "It isn't for us to be sad today, nor any day, for that matter." I continued with "Dad will be forever with us, individually, in every beat of our hearts." I couldn't get the words out of my mouth before a flood of tears and emotions took me over. My siblings jumped up as if the house were on fire and wrapped their arms around me. We all cried and hugged. I hadn't meant for that moment to happen. It just did.

Dad's funeral was beautiful. The minister speakers, and everyone associated with organizing it did an excellent job. It was a big funeral (a number of people were there) and there was a groundswell of support for us. Extended family and friends showed up from everywhere. I had friends there from every avenue of my life, as did my brothers and sister. Even our neighbors were there, and of course our cousins, close and distant, as well as our aunts, uncles, etc.

After we arrived at the chapel, my brothers, my sister, and I stayed close to our mom. Cindie and Stephanie stayed close, too. The funeral was going to be very hard on my mom. She had been strong in the days following my dad's passing, but how she would be after the funeral forward was uncertain. All I could think about was how, in her lifetime, my mom had lost her husband, a child, and her parents. She was about to say goodbye to her husband and friend of 40 years. I remember the music and the sermon at the funeral; both were nice. Funerals in the black community can be an event. There is always music, and there is always the word (scripture reading) and it is always appropriate. For Dad there was a fair bit of crying and sadness, but for the most part, everyone was okay.

In the black community, funerals are referred to as home goings, because the deceased has gone on to be with the Lord. And while that may be true, funerals also serve as reunions. There are many reconnections made by people who have lost touch with each other but are brought together by attending a funeral. After the service, we went to the burial site for a gravesite service and then on to the repast.

I remember having a headache after the funeral services and telling my grandmother (my dad's mom) about the headache. She advised me to drink some hot coffee with salt in it. Nah… I think not.

After the funeral my was not gone. He had not been dead more than two weeks when I received a visit from him. I was with my mom at her house one afternoon. I had gone into what was my sister's old bedroom, and I was laying on one of the beds in the room. It was midday and I was napping. I saw a vision of my dad in the backyard. He was descending a few steps that lead from an upper part of the grassy yard into my mom's patio. He was wearing a brown and gold shirt that I liked, with khaki pants. He was clear as day, and I kept my eyes open, dreaming so he wouldn't go away.

He stayed still, looking at me; looking at him through a glass door leading from my sister's bedroom to the patio. We starred at each other for a few minutes, me lying still on the bed, him standing still, and then he was gone. Then, I opened my eyes. The sun shone brightly outside and I could hear nature clearly, but my dad was not there. Indeed, he was gone.

I can't say honestly that my dad has ever come back after that visit to see me, but I do know he came that day. I guess he knew of my pain from his passing and came back to show me and to let me know he was okay.

If anyone were to ask me, how well I knew my dad, or to describe the relationship I had with him, my answer would be, that I knew him well and we had a good, if not great, relationship. But the truth is probably a mixed bag, slightly more nuanced. I knew the man only so much. When I reflect on him and all that he was as a man and as my father, I realize that there was much more to him than the man I called Dad.

He was my mom's husband, the first real boyfriend she had (they met when she was 15), and the father of her children. He was a decorated war veteran of the Korean conflict, and he was the third of six children who survived child birth born to my grandparents. He was a Master Mason of 32nd Degree Prince Hall, a skilled machinist, and a church deacon. He also played baseball, and he was a Democrat, homeowner, a husband, a brother, an uncle, a cousin, a neighbor, a friend, Myron's dad, Greg's dad, Val's dad, Gerald's dad, my dad, and more.

Eyes open

I reflect with assumptions, suspicions, accuracy, and detail. I am also older today than my dad when he passed away. Some say he died unexpectedly "in the natural." That is , granting some leeway for those who believe in a higher power, such as God, Allah, Buddha, Hindi, Jehovah, or another. I've heard it said that he lived exactly as long as he was supposed to. Some people say God called him home. But I don't believe God called him home. He was at home when he died. I don't believe God ends life unexpectedly, and I don't believe God ends life, period. I do believe that a series of connected events can cause you a physical death, and that is exactly what happened in my dad's case. A series of events directly connected to his health at the time lead to his physical death. I do believe in GOD, and my faith is the very thing that sustains my life. But I would be the first to say that I don't believe the thought processes of people who say God needed him home and that is why my dad is not here today. My mother needed him, his children needed him, and his grandchildren, and other family members and friends needed him, all of them reasons for him to be here today. I miss him all the way down to my bone marrow and I search for him in all that I am, and in my siblings and my mom. I look for signs of life from him in the hopes of being able to say "Hello" again, or "I love you and I realize the sacrifices you made taking care of us, and I really hope you are okay today."

For 12,736 days, or 34 years, 10 months, and 13 days, I called Lovie McDee McClain, "Dad." In all the years he was alive, I never called him anything but that. The word fit him. It wasn't overly snug or loose with him; it just fit, like a favorite pair of jeans. It's funny to me today, because my kids have called me everything from "Dad," to "Kenny," "Pops," and "Daddio." He was just "Dad" to me. He liked to laugh, and did, as often as the material or subject matter allowed for it. But I think he kept his funny side close to the vest and only family members and close friends got to see that side of him. He was comfortable with being serious and reflective. It could be that this character choice, was appropriate for the way in which he grew up.

I was at a movie theatre one afternoon. I was waiting in line for the box office to open. In front of me was an older woman who appeared to be the age of my parents. She had a young boy with her, who I thought might be her grandchild. At one point, the woman turned around and looked in my direction; I saw her face and she saw mine. A minute or more went by before the woman got out of line and approached me. The first thing she said to me was. "You must be a McClain." I said, "Yes, I am," and she replied "You must be Lovie's son," I repeated, "Yes, I am." She introduced herself and said she grew up with my father in Arkansas, knew him well, and sharecropped with him in high school. She also told me I bore a strong resemblance to him. I was very welcoming of her conversation and appreciative of the words. What stuck out most to me was that this was the first I had heard about my dad share-cropping. In all the time he was alive, he never shared those stories with me.

The Spark

Dad had a lot of responsibility early in his life. After his stint in the Marine Corps. he returned to Milwaukee, Wisconsin where he met my mom years earlier. They married soon after he returned from the military. He was 22, and she was 19. Only two years after they were married, they were parents. In less than another two years, they were parents again. They bought their first house soon after. So, things happened very rapidly for them with marriage, kids, and a home. This probably sounds like a normal chain of events for a young couple experiencing adulthood and family life. However, it was also new and a bit of a challenge for my parents, as they migrated from their home states to California. It was there that they settled into life and began to have a family. Both of my parents hailed from the south. Dad was from Arkansas and my mom originally from Mississippi, and later, Wisconsin. Life in the South and the Midwest in early 1950s was far different from life in California at that time. The 1950s saw America 85 years removed from slavery, but the South acted as if it never got the news. Conditions for black people had always been worse in the South than anywhere else in the country. There was Jim Crow, and any and every bias one could dream up against black (Colored or Negro, at the time) people. California, at least on the surface was welcoming and promising.

My dad had not been honorably discharged from the U.S. Marines for long when he received a phone call from his older brother telling him to move west to California. My uncle had been in the Navy, and at the completion of his service, had been discharged in California. He had spent some time there prior to the end of his service, liked what he experienced, and decided he'd stay. He then found work immediately, in the aircraft industry, supporting and supplying aircraft parts to the U.S. Department of Defense. The commercial and defense aircraft industry was very busy at the time, and my uncle relayed that information to my dad.

So, Dad went west and found work immediately. He apprenticed as a machinist until he became skill certified. Initially, my mom didn't work. They were still discovering life, having just gotten married only a couple of years out of youth. As I mentioned earlier within 4 years of being married, they had two kids, me and my brother, Myron, and they were soon to buy a home. Coming from this legacy I hope that I represent what they wanted in a son. It might seem as though it's an un-necessary thought or wish, but it isn't.

One Saturday morning, I sat in a well-known barbershop waiting my turn to have a haircut. The barber was the father of a friend of mine, someone I'd known most of my life. Mr. John Doe knew me well and had watched me grow up with his son. During my haircut, he confided information that was painful for him. Painful was his description of the information. He said to me, "My son is not the kind of kid any father would want to have." He further stated that he was completely disappointed in his son and how he had turned out. I found myself at a loss for words. How was I to comfort this man? I still knew his son well and knew the troubles he spoke about regarding his son. Adding to it was the fact that his son was an only child.

My dad has been gone a long time, but I do stop to wonder if he thought I represented him well. Today, 28 years after his death, I think that because of my almost daily interactions with my dad during his life, I knew him well enough that he would be proud of me and my siblings. I believe he would want us to meet each day with an expectation of excellence. He would hope for us to meet challenges head on. He would hope we would be centered by something greater than ourselves, but he would not push one thing over another. And he would not be supportive of guilt-ridden or obsessive behavior, so I know he would not want us to live a guilt-filled life, based on unfulfilled potential, un-met expectations, or purposeful actions detrimental to ourselves. No, my dad would want me to learn from my mistakes, realize my potential, and meet my expectations head on. At no time would he be disappointed, drone on about nothing, or feel embarrassment about me or my siblings. We were loved unconditionally by our father, and I embrace what I've always known, and that is, that aside from my mother, his children were his greatest achievements.

My father had a huge personality and was arguably the most important man in my life. He loved life, he loved living, and he loved his family. In turn, he was loved back. He was a strict parent; raised in the South in a strict household by a strong mother and father who, no doubt, taught their children skills and behaviors to keep them safe (because of the times) as well as manners infused with Southern tendencies.

I did not get a chance to meet my paternal grandfather. His name was Marshall McDee McClain. My dad and my grandfather shared middle names. My grandfather stood about 6 2" in height, was an average weight for his height, and worked most of his life, up until the day of his passing. He died in his sleep. I'm told he was an easy-going man, polite, and quick to smile and nod, at you and he had large hands, the kind of hands that had seen lots of work. I know he did a lot of rail work, and for a time, his family traveled with him. I'm not certain about the specifics, but I was told this in a conversation with one of my aunts. My grandfather visited California once, when I was very young, but I don't remember that visit. One of my uncles is the spitting image of my grandfather.

My uncle Kirby shares the same face, height and body type as him. But the similarities end there. My uncle (and I love him dearly) is nothing like his father in personality. Maybe his charm is similar, but my uncle uses his charm for mischievous gain, while my grandfather did not.

I did know my paternal grandmother. She was all of 5 0" and 110 pounds soaking wet, but and I'd bet my house mortgage on her in a fight with Mike Tyson. She was a serious woman, or as they say in the African American community, she could turn up on you in no time flat. My dad was afraid of his mom, and he was double her body weight. She could be as sweet as a summer peach, but when they say hell hath no fury like a woman, I know exactly what is meant. I heard my grandmother issue stern warnings to her grown children, my aunts, uncles, and dad, at a time when they were each between 40 and 60 years of age. I know it was out of respect that they obeyed her to the letter, but I think they feared her, too. Fear of the unknown does motivate. As I think about my grandmother, I think it's possible she had a bit of Medea (Tyler Perry's character) in her, and for all I know, she could have been packing. I do know that I did whatever she asked me to do, and I did it with the quickness, or tmmediately (with a T). I witnessed her go upside my cousin's head a couple of times, and that was enough for me. At any rate, my grandparents rubbed off on my dad and his approach to parenting.

Breathe

Our house ran pretty much like any household. At some point, both my parents worked, but my mom cooked dinner almost every night, and on the rare occasions she did not cook, my dad cooked or we ate out. Personally, I preferred the restaurants or take out over my dad's cooking, but I never said anything. We ate dinner with the family around the dinner table most evenings; the meal was a staple in our house when I was young. I also grew up with chores, rules, and expectations. There were consequences for unmet chores and expectations. Early on my parents believed in corporal punishment- translation – ass whooping's - but as they grew and matured and had more children, they moved pass that groundings, talks, or shunning you out of your ignorance. Every act of discipline on the part of my parents was meant to teach us betterment. We were never punished out of frustration or as a relief from parenting. Whatever punishment we received was duly earned.

My mom and dad admonished us about certain things during our childhood, but the admonishments were all about teaching respect, and a appropriate behavior. We were taught to respect our elders. We said "Mr." and "Mrs.", "Yes madam" and "No sir." We also say "Thank you," "You're welcome," "Please and May I." We did not call people liars, we did not cuss, we did not say "Shut up," and we did not answer with a "Yeah," or "Nah." The aforementioned behavior was not taught to us; therefore, it was not tolerated. My dad was the enforcer when discipline was needed, but my mom did sometimes correct our behavior if it was needed. My mother would defer to my dad if an infraction was serious or if she felt we were not responding to her discipline. We would be told ahead of time that the incident was going to be referred to my dad. The notice was really a warning that an ass whooping was on the way. My dad did not relish giving us corrective discipline, but when he did, he would spring into action like an MMA fighter, and our asses would be lit up! He made sure each lesson got through to us, because he would talk to us the whole time, we were getting the ass whooping.

When my dad died as he did, suddenly and without warning, my life unraveled. I realized I didn't have answers for the questions now immediately in front of me, questions concerning all avenues of adulthood. Yes, I was a grown man with a new family; however, I had never been without the counsel of my dad, and I was faced with making decisions without the shadow of my father in the background and dealing with the aftermath of those decisions. My dad never forced his opinions or his counsel on me. He regarded me as a grown man, and as such, he enjoyed new conversations that came as a result of my adulthood. Nevertheless, I always knew my dad's reasoning, counsel, and good judgement were available to me if and when I needed them. I had no reasonable explanation that I could fully understand for why my dad died the way he did. I had not heard mention anything concerning an issue with his heart. This unraveling of my life happened bit by bit, steadily over time. When change takes place at a slow but steady pace, it is difficult to detect. When I gave this idea additional thought, I concluded the following. Most often, when un-suspected change is occurs in our lives, if we sense its occurrence and we recognize that the change is gradual, we generally assign an attitude of procrastination to any self-adjustments that need to be made. We consciously neglect ourselves. In other words, we put off the self-work needed to prevent or mitigate a disastrous outcome. In these situations, we are rarely, if ever, right in our assessments.

If you are fortunate enough to draw breath into your body in a new day, then you had better show up to live in the day granted to you. I did show up, every day. I was forced to live during a time I was mourning; nevertheless, time does not stand still, and I had to stay rationale. My family was supportive, which helped. I did find myself acting and behaving in ways counter to how I would have if my dad had still been alive. Without him and his ability to buffer my juvenile temptations, I began living without self-restraint, responsibility, and boundaries. This is all in retrospect. Had I known, or been more self-aware, I believe I would have tried, at a minimum, to help myself. When my father was alive, boundaries both real and imagined were respected. He had been my guard-rail without me ever knowing it. His steadfastness with me was as present when I was 34 years as it was when I was six. Nevertheless, with his passing, those boundaries took on less meaning. You do not know what you do not know until you come face to face with an inability to fend for yourself. I was not aware that I had lost focus, but began to realize clearly when, during a conversation with my ex-wife, after our divorce, she said "We would have never gotten divorced if your father were still living." There is something about the truth when you hear it; it just feels right, and it rings right in your ears.

In the aftermath of my self-destruction, I had bouts of despondency, depression, and anger. I believed that I deserved the worst life experience imaginable. At times, I felt I owed it to myself to have negative thoughts about myself. I held myself hostage with feelings that were negative towards me. I denied myself any positive affirmations or suggestions of adequacy, because I believed I did not deserve anything positive. The one thing that held me together was my beautiful daughter, Stephanie, and how much I loved her; I did not want to let her down.

At some point, the unraveling of my life stopped, and rationale thinking returned. I made a self-analysis, and what I came up with was that I had let myself and my family down, and because of that, was an outcast, put more simply, a complete failure. A lot had gone wrong in a short period of time. I was divorced, I had found and loss a second relationship, I had loss some friends and was stuck in a dead-end job. I was living far below the bar established by my own standards. My dad would have been displeased. His expectations for me were not over-achievement, nor were his expectations unachievable. My father's wishes and expectations came from knowing his kids, interacting with them every day, and learning what each of us was capable of on our own. He felt that if you did not match your goal to your talent, then you were only letting yourself down.

To my immediate knowledge, my father did not know the meaning of the word "quit." The way he lived his life, you'd almost believe he discarded the word from his vocabulary. He had no quit in him as far as I know. Maybe he had challenges I was unaware of, and maybe my mom knew his weaknesses better than I did, or at least I imagine she did, but I did not know of any challenges he had. Moreover, I never knew him to give up on anything.

Finding Courage

I have given up plenty, and I know myself to be a quitter. During my darkest of times, I thought about ending my life. I also made attempts but I was unsuccessful. Life's challenges had gotten the best of me, and I gave up. Today, I understand that the challenges I faced were brought on by me, by decisions I made, and without understanding them, consequences would circle back as a result.

These were periods of time during which my pain was excruciating. Emotional pain manifested into physical and psychological pain. I tried. I tried. But every attempt at normalcy and an everyday life seemed to be too much for me. The act of suicide is not a spontaneous act; it's deliberate, premeditated, and carefully planned. It is after much thought that one ends his or her life. I did that-the planning part. I thought about it and thought about it and only after concluding I could not live with the pain anymore, I tried to end it. You understand fully that in ending the pain you are also ending your life, but that is the bargain and the price is agreed to in advance. I failed at each attempt (I made 2) and only after interventions did - I realize I could go on. I could keep living. I could manage the pain. And I did continue, I am still here, and the pain is gone. The details of my attempts, i.e, the means I employed are not important. But I reveal this information to say that as difficult as challenges can be, my dad never showed a weakness connected to such an attempt. If he failed at something, at least, he failed putting forth an attempt.

My father stressed education, and he stressed the importance of becoming educated. All the time, he used to say to me, "A blind man can dig a ditch." It was more than an analogy; he sought to get through to me that to do anything outside of average and ordinary would require being educated. He did not, however, stress school. The thing was, my dad, a realist, understood that people learn in different ways, and that one could become educated by means other than the perceived conventional method, i.e., high school, college, or another form of formal education. He did not knock school, but he understood that becoming educated was a result of endless curiosity, and sometimes, you could learn outside conventional means. The important thing my dad taught was that you needed to be educated enough to take care of yourself in all situations.

The ability to communicate was high on this list of must-haves. He stressed accurate and clear communication. He also stressed self-reliance and accountability. My parents were both from the South and they knew the struggle for equality well, especially for people of color, and they knew the relevance of personal sacrifice. They hoped to instill in us a sense of urgency regarding a responsible approach to life and living.

Dad's imprint on our lives was consistent. He was a physical presence in my day-to-day life from the time I was born. He was there while I grew up, got married, became a father, and bought a home. This was a welcome presence that loomed large. Contrary to the stereotype of black men always leaving, my dad stayed. He and my mom were married and together, as marital vows go, "til death do them part." I guess you could say their union was meant to be, and we, their children, were the beneficiaries of the stability brought to us through their shared sacrifices. When someone has been in your life as provider, caretaker, stabilizer, and all the other roles that parents play, it can be easy to take for granted all that is being done for you. But people make choices, and my dad chose to be a father. He did not leave, and he wasn't hands off; he engaged and participated in the everyday struggle that was parenting. He and my mom sacrificed, went without, over spent, and did all that they could to make certain that their four children had the necessities. But we did not have only the basics; we had more and then some. For example, my parents saw to it that us three played little league baseball. I know it sounds simple, but consider entrance fees for three boys, as well as uniform fees, including gloves, and shoes, going to and from practice every week, going to game days and everything else. We also had health insurance, (we visited the doctor for regular scheduled physical exams), we went to the dentist, we went on school field trips, and so on. My sister had the same experience; she was in Girl Scouts, she went to the beauty salon, and on extra outings, and more.

I regret my transgressions. I regret allowing my life to spiral downwards. I lost my moral footing, my stability, and even my confidence. In making these statements, I acknowledge that a day is not promised, and I acknowledge that during the time I was able to spend with my dad, he taught me and ushered me to responsibility such that his lessons would be sustaining no matter the amount of time we had together. It was as if I were given a check book, and he knew there was enough in the bank to cover any check written. But, as the Bible says, a fool and his money are soon parted. I blew it, all of it. My mom did her job holding the family together after my dad's passing. And I acknowledge her role in shared parenting. However, mothers and fathers are different in what they give a child. Even if and when both parents are on the same page, espousing the same message, the instruction from the father comes across differently to the child. Call it the deeper voice syndrome or mustache versus no mustache, fathers are received differently than mothers. Fathers are more likely to offer what I refer to as bottom-line parenting. When the father is an every-day parent, on the scene from start to finish, his decisions, corrections, discipline, encouragement, and other contributions to a child can, (purposely or not) drive out ambiguity and strengthen and mold certainty in his child. I did not realize this complete impact my dad had on me in my growth to manhood and my overall stability as a person until years after his passing.

In a short space of time after the death of my dad, one setback was all that happened before I began to experience anger issues. The actual evidence of this is not something you could get me to admit to. I had sensed the anger in myself on several occasions. I became angry even with the most trivial things. Why the anger appeared I'm not sure, and I don't know from where it originated. I never had an anger issue that I was aware of before the passing of my dad. I'm not sure now how the anger in my life led me or failed me in handling sensitive or difficult issues I faced. I guess what can be said with honesty is that I am not certain that my anger connected directly to the death of my dad. I am a passionate person, and I always have been, but when these troubles arose, I went beyond mere passion directly to emotional venting. I still wonder today even if there is a connection between my dad's death and my anger issue. I know of and have spoken with people who have acknowledged they had anger after the death of a parent. Some even went so far as to say life is unfair. I do believe I behaved in the same way. And as far as I know, I did not assign an overall unfairness to life in a broad and general sense.

I do recall tapping into a reservoir of anger and not knowing how deep the well went. In my opinion, when I did access something other than my smiley face, displeasure, for example, what I chose to exhibit warranted and probably overdue. Nonetheless, I am stating my opinion. I am not out of control with anger or volatility. But I will admit there has been a time or two when I acted or behaved beyond acceptability. Even I know as much.

However, I have grown tired, and fed-up with the notion that political correctness is the right behavior in all instances. The problem I have with political correctness for all situations is that it is often used as one of the new forms of institutionalized racism against, or oppression of people like me: black men. I consider myself a responsible being. I know how to comport myself. However, if I am in a situation and it begins to go left and spiral out of control, I am to follow PC guidelines. This expectation is where I have a problem. Political correctness keeps me and those like me, people of color, docile and diplomatic, even when we are under attack. I believe strongly that if you can solve an issue diplomatically, then you should use that platform until it is exhausted. But if, you have to tell someone to take a hike and you need to do so using colorful language, then so be it.

My dad lent structure to everything. And he earned his designation of "Dad" not just because he was my biological donor, no, he showed up day in and day out and put in the work. My dad allowed us to make mistakes. I know this because I made plenty, and he rarely made a fuss about them. I've come to know he wanted us to learn from them; thus, he was hesitant to quickly correcting them. [A side note: my dad also possessed a wicked sense of humor. It wasn't often on display, but when it was, it was wicked and his comedic timing was impeccable.]

When I think about my dad and all that he provided, I am acutely aware that I am also a part of a parenting system in which my dad was an active participant. My parents provided a home, stability, encouragement, hope, discipline, fortitude, humor, integrity, truthfulness, and more. As a father, although not perfect, I'm 100% committed to ensuring my children get a quality education, have food to eat, receive medical care, and, at a minimum, obtain the attributes necessary to succeed on their own. Considering this, I'm incensed at the thought of the narrow minded, negative, and untrue narrative of the black man as a failure in marriage and fatherhood. Most of my black male friends are dads, and concerned with every aspect of our children's lives.

Black men care for their children as any or most parents do. We love, teach, provide, discipline, prod, urge, and nod, all in the direction of excellent health and well-being. Mistakes are inevitable, but a deliberant avoidance of parental responsibility is not something I am familiar with, nor does it apply to any black men in my circle of friends. Why I even have to say as much is puzzling to me.

Thursday

My father's heart attack occurred in the early morning hours of October 25th, 1990, and he died almost immediately. The time was 5:00 am. It was Thursday.

Earlier that month, two big things happened for my family. First, my wife and I closed escrow on a house. The house had a drive of approximately three to five minutes to where my parents lived. Second, my daughter turned three that year. There was a lot of joy and jubilation early in the month. In the middle of the jubilation, there were signs, not clearly obvious, indicating danger on the horizon; they were there for me to read, and I didn't. The signs were signaling that father's time on this earth was nearing its end. I simply did not know, at the time, how to read the signs.

My dad and I had unspoken, playful form of communication that would play out nearly 100% of the time when I'd go to visit my parents at their home. I'd knock on the door or ring the doorbell, and my dad would answer and ask if my daughter was with me. Most of the time, she was, and as she was used to her grandfather and his playful nature, so she'd hide behind me, giggling, or sometimes stand to the side of the door, where she would be hidden when he opened it. When I'd tell him that she was with me, he'd step outside, find her, and pick her up taking her away from me, then turn and walk back through the door into the house. He'd head straight into a den, where my mother would be waiting. They'd take turns entertaining their granddaughter. I'd be left to make my way into the house on my own. My daughter Stephanie was the only grandchild at the time, and my parents had no apology for spoiling her as they did. The door habit was routine.

Maybe a week before his passing, his interactions with me took a strange and noticeable twist. I'd come over, and I'd knock on the door or ring the doorbell as before, only he'd open the door and just stare at me. He did not ask if Stephanie was with me, and he did not step outside to find her, pick her up, and go inside; instead, he'd just stand there and stare. The first couple times this happened, I didn't say anything, but the third time, said, playfully, "Move outta my way, man" or something to that effect. He was behaving as if he was in a trance, having senior moments or memory lapses. After maybe 10 seconds, he'd get some clarity, snap back to alertness, and, move to allow me entry into the house. Those 10 seconds were noticeable. I also noticed my dad, on occasion, would stare or look at me as if he were seeing me for the first-time when we'd sit together. This happened while we were sitting on the den sofa watching television, or during casual conversation. He'd just stare and stare.

I was reading the autobiography of a very famous musician whose work I admire, and in his autobiography, there is his account of an experience he had with his mother, that was the same as what I experienced with my dad. The musician had gone to visit his mother, who lived in another state. During the visit, he noticed her giving him long stares and quiet moments of just looking at him. He noticed the behavior, but at the time it was happening, he said nothing and thought nothing. He returned to his home after the visit, and shortly thereafter, his mother passed away. Reflecting on the visit, he surmised that his mother's spirit was trying to tell him goodbye. He felt guilt ridden that he had not noticed her very deliberate attempts to reach him. I think (and I am guessing here), his guilt stemmed from being disconnected to his sensitivity at the time. Artists are generally very aware and usually have high EQs.

They also, they tend to be keen observers of behavior. The inability to discern his mother's odd behavior and question it her passing was an upsetting experience for him. But again, I am guessing at this. I connected with the sentiment immediately. I know this was happened and I know it wasn't all in my mind. I know my dad's behavior with me in the last days of his life were far different than normal. Like the musician, I've come to believe his spirit was saying goodbye, and I just didn't pick up on it. I'd heard of incidents of this kind occurring before. There have been first-hand accounts of people who witnessed what they believed to be spirit phenomena at the time people passed away.

The day before my dad's passing, Wednesday, October 24th 1990, played out the same as any other day. I went to work, and at the end of my day, I drove to a child-care facility to pick up my daughter; she attended a combination preschool and day care. Normally, I was there at around 5:30 p.m. each day. My wife worked nights as a registered nurse at Children's Hospital in Los Angeles, California. She worked a 7 p.m. to 7 a.m. shift three days a week, and one eight-hour shift on the weekends. My wife dropped Stephanie off at preschool day care at some hour in the morning and I picked her up on my way home from work each day. I loved it.

Some of the happiest moments of my life are walking through the door and surprising my baby girl. She'd be excited and run to me to be picked up, hugged, and kissed. She was a deserving princess. We'd get into the car and head home. We lived a short distance from where she attended preschool day care, near my parents' house. Because we lived near my mom and dad, most nights, Stephanie and I would stop at their house to say hi and give my parents a chance to interact with their only grandchild. My father would beam at the sight of Stephanie, and he wanted to hold her and play games with her non-stop. Plus, some nights,

Stephanie and I ate dinner at their house, thus relieving me of the responsibility preparing dinner for Stephanie and myself.

On October 24th, 1990, we drove in the usual direction but we did not stop at my parents' house. We drove directly home. Why, I don't know. When we arrived home, I did something unusual. I backed the car into the driveway, instead of driving head in, and not only did I do this, but I also stopped the car midway down the driveway. After, I got out of the car and opened our gate, which was in the middle of the driveway at the front of the house, so I could move the car all the way back to our detached garage. I never did that; this was the first time. I did not even question why I was doing this; I just did it. Then we got out of the car, and I opened the back door to let us into the kitchen. I turned off the house alarm, and Stephanie and I went in. We did the usual stuff- we grabbed some dinner, and watched a little television, then Stephanie had a bath and I got her into her pajamas and put her to bed between 8:00 and 8:30 p.m. I stayed awake and watched the news, as I did most nights, before closing up the house and going to bed myself after 11p.m. Stephanie was three, so didn't sleep through the night. It wasn't unusual for her to call out in the middle of the night and ask if she could get into bed with me. Her behavior was the same when her mom was home, too. We'd say yes, and, on this night, when she called out, I said yes, and she crawled into bed with me around 2:00 a.m.

At around 4:30 a.m. the phone rang. It was the house phone, and we had one that sat on a night- stand next to the bed. I answered, and it was my mom, frantic. She was yelling for me to get to the house there was a problem with my dad. I remember I didn't panic. I hung the phone up and sat on the edge of the bed, thinking for a minute. At around age 55, my dad had developed adult onset asthma. I figured he was having an asthma attack, and I knew my mom would stabilize him and he'd be okay. At the end of that thought, the phone rang again, only this time, it was my brother, and he, too, was frantic and yelling: "Kenny! Get down here; it's Dad!" I could tell he was scared. His voice screamed panic and chaos. I jumped out of bed, threw on some slippers, and grabbed Stephanie in the blankets that were on the bed. I ran out the back door with Stephanie in my arms, opened the car door, and placed Stephanie on the back seat. I jumped into the driver's seat, ready to go. As fate would have it, I had backed my car into the driveway, and now it was ready to go. At 4:45 a.m., we raced toward my parents' house. The three-minute drive was achieved in only one minute. I thought of nothing as I drove as fast as possible.

As I turned onto their street, I was met with lights from a fire truck, at least three sheriff cars, an ambulance, and lots of neighbors in front of my parent's house in their pajamas. I parked my car directly across the street from their house. The way the street was laid out, the public vehicles were all in a clump. As I was exited my car, one of the neighbors, Mrs. Hodges, came to my car door. She placed her knee against the driver's side door, blocking me from exiting the car. She said, "Kenny, it's your father, and it doesn't look good." I said "Okay," she repeated what she said, and again I said, "Okay." I was told my father and mother were both in the ambulance. A few of the neighbors had gone inside the house to calm my brother. I went inside and found my brother crying. I assured him things would be okay, and told him I was going to follow the ambulance to the hospital, and I'd return once things got normal. He said okay, and many of the neighbors said they'd stay with him.

From the noise and confusion around the car, Stephanie had woken up and was sitting up in the backseat when I returned. I was out of the car for fewer than five minutes. Stephanie asked if everything was okay, and I told her that Papa was sick, we were going to follow an ambulance to the hospital to make sure everything was okay. In fact, the ambulance left the scene minutes earlier, when I went into the house to check on my brother.

Stephanie and I raced towards Huntington Memorial Hospital, where the ambulance was taking my dad. We arrived just minutes after the ambulance. I parked on the street just outside of the emergency parking. One of the ambulance attendees came out of the hospital, back to the ambulance to get something. I asked, "How's the patient," he seemed startled, then said, he didn't know and I was going to have to ask the doctor. I said, "C'mon man, please tell me something; that's my dad in there." He relented and told me that my dad had a pulse, but was barely breathing. He seemed sad and concerned. I thanked him.

Stephanie and I went into the hospital and found my mom. She was very upset and unable to talk. Soon after, my dad's brothers and sisters arrived. I guessed my mom had made some calls. My dad's siblings who lived in the area all showed up to the hospital. We sat together, waiting to hear from the doctors. The room was quiet-still, actually-with everyone in thought and prayer. We were in the hallway of the emergency center. Huntington Hospital was outstanding, equipped with the latest technology and some of the finest medical professionals in the country. Its sterile smell permeated the hallway where we sat. One of my aunts, my father's younger sister, was upset, she kept saying, "No, no, not my brother," and pacing up and down the hall.

A doctor finally emerged through a door. His face was expressionless as he made eye contact with us. He asked if we were all together for patient McClain, and we said we were. As there were seven of us, he wanted to find a small room where he could address us. He found a room, and all of us, except my Aunt Mae, went. We sat in a semicircle and the doctor pulled up a very small round stool and sat. In a very quiet, calm voice, he announced, "Mr. McClain has had a heart attack." And then he paused. The room was quiet. My mom replied, quietly asking "What do we do now?" The doctor spoke calmly: "There is nothing else that can be done. He passed away."

The silence in the room was deafening. It was as if time had stopped completely, and we were all frozen in place. That silence, that moment-the stillness with which we existed-in the moment was broken after a full minute, followed by a chorus of crying. Everyone in the room cried at once, except Stephanie and me. I didn't know it at the time, but I was in shock. I sat still with her on my lap, not saying a word. There isn't any other way to explain my behavior. My mom, my aunt Myrlean, and my two uncles, Lee and Pete were all crying uncontrollably. My Aunt Mae, outside the room heard the noise and ran in. When she was told her brother had passed away, she too began to cry. My dad and his sisters were close, and their crying and pain were matched only by the crying and pain my mother was suffering in the moment. I was sitting opposite the doctor. He (bless him), showed great poise and was very respectful. He looked at me and asked if I was my dad's son, and I said yes. He told me, "Your father went without any pain," and asked if he could show me something, I said yes. He began to demonstrate with his hands how the heart pumps, and he explained what happens when there is an interruption, or heart attack, of the magnitude my dad suffered. He said, "The person initially feels a small discomfort in their chest, and then nothing." He seemed very concerned about everyone in the room, and I tried to alleviate some of his discomfort by engaging in conversation with him. He asked me if I'd like to see my dad, to which I said yes. He led me into the emergency room where they had worked on him. My dad lay there, motionless, warm, handsome, and peaceful. He had a tube in his mouth, which I believe they had been using to get air into his lungs. Stephanie asked, "Why does Papa have that tube in his mouth, and why is he sleeping?" I don't know if I gave her an answer or not. I stood still, looking at my dad, and admiring him, not processing that I'd not see him again in this life. I cannot remember if anyone other than myself and Stephanie went into that room. We stayed maybe five minutes, and I believe we were at the hospital for another 30-45 minutes before finally leaving. My mom had come by ambulance with my dad. She was returned to her house, a widow.

My cousin Dewayne passed away at age 32. The primary cause of death was an enlarged heart. I'm not sure of the medical terminology for his condition; it could have been congestive heart failure, but don't quote me on it. His mother, my aunt Jeannie, (my mom's sister), told me, she would routinely go to the hospital every evening and sit with her son as he was being treated for his condition. It was not unusual for my aunt to fall asleep some evenings in a chair sitting beside Dewayne's bed. On the night before he passed away, my aunt said she had fallen asleep in the chair at his bedside, and she was awakened by noise, which she said was definitely an ongoing conversation. She said she woke to find Dewayne sitting straight up in his hospital bed and motioning with his hands for people to come into the room. She looked in the direction of the door, but there was nobody there. However, Dewayne was in full conversation with what appeared to be a group of people. My aunt distinctly remembers Dewayne mentioning "Big Daddy," my grandfather, and her dad, telling him to come into the room. My grandfather had been dead for years. My aunt is adamant in the telling of this story, and nothing suggests to me that she made it up. It suggests Dewayne's spirit had already departed his body, and was engaged with those he knew his and their physical lives. Dewayne's physical death followed the next morning.

A New Normal

R iding home from the hospital in my car were Stephanie, my mom, and my aunt Myrlean, my father's eldest sister. My grandmother, my dad's mom, was at my aunt's house and did not come to the hospital that morning. As we drove toward my aunt's house, the shock of my dad dying wore off, and I was hit right in the face with the reality of his death. I began to cry uncontrollably, causing everyone in the car to start crying. I can say we were a car traveling on the mercy of God because there was no way I could control the car at the rate I was crying. The pain of the loss was excruciating and continuous. I could not believe my dad was gone. I thought "Oh God, please wake me up and tell me this is a terrible dream, because I don't know what I am going to do." My aunt, bless her heart, yelled for me to pull over to the curb. I did. We cried together, all of us in concert. After a few minutes, I pulled myself together enough to make the remainder of the drive home. We arrived at my aunt's house and dropped her off. My mom and I continued a half mile up to her house. It was just her house now. Neighbors were waiting for us to return. When we got there the news of my father's death passed through quickly. Most of them had been awakened by the commotion hours earlier. They took the news hard. My family had been a fixture in the neighborhood for years, and most of the neighbors, if not all of them, knew my mom and dad.

I stayed with my mom and brother because we needed to call my younger brother, Greg, and my sister, Val. I don't remember the details of how we broke the news to Greg, but when I spoke with him, he was devastated. He was close to my dad, and they shared a love of baseball-more than Myron and I had. This was the hardest thing we had to deal with as a family.

Valerie was 16 when my dad passed away, and she had just moved into the dorms at her college as a freshman. The move had happened only a few weeks earlier. My wife, my daughter, Mom, Dad and I moved Val onto campus. I couldn't believe my sister was a freshman in college and about to live away from home. We were proud of her. But in a month's time, her dad died. We called her dorm room and the phone was answered by one of her dorm mates. We asked the young lady to tell Val, that she was needed at home and that she should leave immediately. Val got on the phone and asked if there was anything wrong. We said no, but she was insistent, and looking back, it was stupid to believe she would just jump in the car and drive home without knowing anything. I think we had to tell her that dad had passed away. She sensed something was wrong and pressed to be told the truth, so that she could deal with it, and not be surprised. I imagine it was a sobering drive home for a 16- year-old, trying to navigate morning traffic for 20 miles out of the valley in LA. Val is much younger than us brothers and she grew up under the direct protection of my mom and dad. Both my parents had an intense love for Val. She was the only girl and nine and a half years separated her in age from the nearest brother.

When I was 16, I was a high school junior; the year was 1972. I was running late one morning as I prepared to go to school. Our school bus was going to be arriving soon, and I was no-where near ready. I finished dressing, but needed to get into a bathroom near my parents' bedroom. I remember running up the hall leading past their bedroom into the bathroom my natural (afro) needed to be forked out (combed). When I passed my parents' bedroom, I caught a glimpse of my mom starring at herself in the mirror. I didn't say anything, because I had to go, and I was running late. As I exited the bathroom, my mother yelled out to me to come back. I yelled back that I had to go because I was running late, and I needed to get to the bus stop to catch the bus. My mom said, "Get back here, boy, and see what I want." I reluctantly went back. She was just standing there, looking at herself still in the mirror, when she said, "I'm pregnant; I'm going to have a baby." I yelled, "WHAT?". She laughed and said, "I said, I'm pregnant, and I'm going to have a baby in a few months." "Oh shit." Envisioning your parents' still having sex is not what you want on the day of your Algebra test. I asked, "What the hell is going on with you and dad at night." My mom, was beaming, and what I hadn't wrapped my head around was the fact that my mom was only 37 years old at the time. I don't know if I had ever seen her so happy. She had already had four boys, and I imagine she was hoping, praying, and willing for that child to be a girl. After a bit of small talk, I left the house headed for school.

As the time grew near for my mother to have the baby in November, my grandmother flew out to stay with us. Big Momma, my mom's mother, was so sweet. She loved us kids and called all of us "baby," and did all the sweet grandmother stuff. She was there to help my mom and dad around the house once the baby arrived. Doctors at that time were not as able to tell the sex of a child as they are today. Parents would be just as surprised as anyone in the delivery room at the sex of their child at the delivery. Even the due date was less of an educated guess than it is today. One day when I went to school, and when I returned home and my grandmother was in the kitchen, laughing and talking with my dad. I asked what happened, and they told me that my mom had given birth to a healthy baby girl. My parents named her Valerie. I had a sister – Val.

Time flew, and 16 years later, I recall my dad asking me to ride with him to take my sister Val to her high school year book editor's meeting in the mountains at Arrow Head. A very sweet memory for me is watching my dad and sister hug it out before we dropped her for the weekend. It was a very dear dad and daughter moment. My father loved his only daughter. He might have been more excited and happier at the sight of her than my mom. He was sentimental that way. I still hold that picture of my dad and my sister in my memory today.

After we told Val that dad died and asked her to come home, I noticed the time; it was approaching 7:00 am. I knew my wife, Cindie, would be home from work soon. I decided to leave my daughter at my mom's while I drove up to our house to tell my wife that my dad had just passed away. I arrived at my house and went inside. My wife, just home herself, was startled at seeing me. She was generally tired after getting home from a 12-hour shift, and I could see she was tired that morning. She could sense something was off and asked if everything was okay. I said, "No it isn't; my dad died this morning." Cindie did not say anything right away. She just seemed to let my words hang there, then turned and walked away. Initially, I didn't know what to think. I thought maybe she didn't hear me. But she had, and she was going to our bedroom to drop her things and head directly to my mom's house. In the days after, I could tell Cindie was hurt by my dad's death. She had a great relationship with him and the news crushed her. She didn't say much, but she didn't have to. I could tell she took the news badly.

Coping

Days, weeks, months, and years have passed since my dad's death. I used to hurt just thinking about him, but those wounds have healed. I still miss him. I miss his jokes and his easy mannerisms. As I said before not many people got to see the joking side of my dad, although I'm certain his close friends knew him to be quite funny, and maybe even a jokester. But we always saw him as somber, serious, and slow to find the funny side of life. I know he kept his funny side hidden. Apparently, he only shared that side of his character with me, his close friends, and a few of my friends. Bernard, a friend of mine, was privy to some of my father's jokes and antics. He'd have me and Bernard cracking up.

Every now and again, I try to retrace my entire relationship with my dad. I know there's sometimes no use in trying, but I've been able to extract some beautiful and not so beautiful moments. I do have some very strong memories of the early 60s and watching the nightly news with my dad, and seeing the devastation of the war in Vietnam. We sat and watched Walter Cronkite and listened to the stories about the fighting, that had taken place that day. We saw lines of body bags filled with the bodies of American soldiers, or whatever parts of them could be collected. My dad watched stoically, never saying anything but never turning away, either. Since he had been in the Korean conflict, and wounded by gunfire, I wondered what he thought about as he sat and watched the news accounts of Vietnam. My dad wasn't overly political, and I cannot say if he voiced opposition or support for the Vietnam war.

Another memory is watching Johnny Carson with my dad. He loved late night television, and he loved Johnny Carson. My dad said the television cemeteries were filled (figuratively) with people going up against Carson and his late-night television show. For my dad, Johnny reigned supreme. He had other favorites on television, too; he loved Flip Wilson and Geraldine, Redd Foxx, The Bill Cosby show, westerns, and clean comedies. I suspect he loved the dirty comedies, too, but he had the moral discipline to eschew "R" rated stuff when we were around. As a matter of fact, I know he liked the more adult themed stuff too, because he had a couple of Mom's Mabley albums.

The last outing, I had with my father was a memorable trip to a baseball game. It was just the two of us. I had two tickets to see the Dodgers play at Dodger Stadium for one of the final games in 1990. I believe it was a mid-September game. I called my dad and asked him if he was interested in going, and he said yes. The Dodgers were my dad's favorite team, and baseball was his favorite sport. So, I drove over to my parents' house with plenty of leeway to get to the game on time. My father was the type of person to be ready long before he needed to be. I don't know if it was just a generational thing or not, but if you told my dad to be ready to go at 6:00 p.m., he was ready and chomping at the bit by 3:30 p.m. By 6:00 p.m., he was exhausted from waiting around to go. So, I got to their house, and of course my dad was ready to go. I could barely say hello to my Mom by the time Dad is saying, "Let's go." So, we took off.

I drove different route than the one I knew my dad would take. I remembered from going someplace a week earlier that there was, "what I thought," an easier way to get to Dodger Stadium, that would avoid most of the game day traffic. I decided to take that route instead of traveling the tried and tested 110 freeway. We were driving in that new direction when my father asked "Where are you going?" I told him that I'd discovered a new way to the stadium, one that avoided most of the game traffic, so he said, "Okay," and settled into the drive. I exited a freeway to a parking lot, traffic jammed up and everyone crawling along. My father looked over at me with a "WTF Kenneth?" expression. I didn't say anything, but tried to weave in and out of the mess the best I could. All around us, everyone had Dodger flags on their cars, and the traffic was, without question, headed to Dodger Stadium the same as us. I had no idea game day would be like that. Where we would have been at least 20 minutes early and in our seats if I had I taken the old standard route, it was approaching the first pitch, and we were still a couple miles out from the stadium. There was still the task of getting to the stadium, parking, and finding our seats. My father was disappointed not so much that he wanted to take it out on me personally, but enough to ask me if I had ever gone to a game using that route before, and to lament that we weren't going to be there until about the 3rd inning. Eventually we got a break and traffic opened for us. We finally made the game at the bottom of the first inning. My dad could not have been happier. We were sitting down the third base line in field box seats, with a great view of the game. We also had Dodger dogs, and cokes. My dad did not drink alcohol, and I generally did not care for beer, so cokes prevailed. It was a great outing, but it was our last.

I wasn't prepared for my father's death, and even if I had been, there is no adequate preparation available when you have to process the death of a loved one. Even if my dad had been ill with a lingering illness, and I had been able to spend every day, all day with him, I don't know or believe I would have been prepared for his passing. You grieve. It is hard. There are tears and longing. And we say and hear all the clichés associated with death after a loved one is gone: "They aren't in pain anymore;" "They're now with others who have gone on before them"-"they" this, and "they" that, whatever. The pain of losing my dad was as if someone had pressed a hot iron against my heart.

My dad's birthday was December 31st, New Year's Eve, and I always found it strange that he did not drink alcohol. We had it in the house, mostly because someone was always giving him a bottle of this or that for Christmas or his birthday. These gifts almost always came from co-workers. I asked my mom once why my dad didn't partake in alcoholic beverages, and she told me a story. One year, I believe 1956 his company had a Christmas office party, and my dad had a brand-new car. His work was very near where they lived at the time. My mom wasn't feeling well the night of the party and opted out, but she encouraged my dad to go. So, he did and he drove his new car. The morning after the party, my dad woke up at the house in bed with my mom, and the first thing he asked was if his car was in the driveway. My mom responded, "Yes." Apparently, my dad drove home drunk, he didn't know how he had gotten home, did not remember driving, and wasn't sure his car was with him. The incident scared him so much that he never drank alcohol again.

Human

My father was not one to reveal troubling times, nor did he spend any time that I could remember claiming to be a victim of anything. Okay, there was an occasional disagreement with my mom, or I would hear some grumbling about something that had happened at work. There were also occasional disagreements with extended family, which is inherent in every family, but largely, my dad remained quiet about personal challenges. There were, however, three distinct times that I know of when my father was pained, and those three times are seared into my memory. Once he told me, and the other two I witnessed. Seeing my dad in pain was much more difficult than listening to him describe an incident that was hard for him. The first incident I witnessed happened late one night. I shared a bedroom with my two brothers, Myron and Greg. We loved the room; there was a set of bunk beds on one wall, and I slept in the top bunk, while my youngest brother Greg, slept on the bottom bunk. Myron slept in a full-sized bed on the opposite wall. We'd get into the room at night, and Myron and I would scare the crap out of Greg with wild stories or some made up boogeyman hocus pocus. Other times, the three of us would be in the room laughing and cracking jokes until either my mom or my dad would come to the door and threaten to kill us and bury our bodies in the back yard.

We were in bed one night when I heard a loud noise, like a low groan, and then a thud, like something hitting the floor, followed by crying. The crying was scary to me at the time, because it was more like a continuous wailing. Initially, I could not make out who was crying. I knew the only other people in the house with us, were my mom and dad. After the thought, I heard my mom's voice; she was talking to someone. The crying continued. I climbed down from my bed, and walked towards the hallway. I could see there was a light on in the hallway. It was late, probably near 11:00 p.m. or thereabouts. I could see my father was lying on the floor of the hallway, crying. My mother, who was on the phone, looked up, saw me, and continued to talk. At the time, we had two rotary phones in the house, one in our hallway and one on a wall in the kitchen. On the phone with my mother was my aunt Myrlean, my dad's older sister. She had called to tell my dad that my grandfather was dead.

My grandfather had died in his sleep earlier that day. I don't know why we got the news so late afterwards. The story I heard was that my grandmother had woke that morning and started off the day as any other. She had gone into the kitchen to prepare breakfast for my grandfather. He did not wake at what was his normal time come breakfast, and while it was unusual, it was not so out of character to cause alarm. However, after some time, when he did not wake, my grandmother went to check on him and found he was already gone.

My dad was devastated. My grandfather was a mountain of a man who was beloved by many in and out of the family. He had a very nurturing way, and my dad was extremely fond of him. It appeared his whole world had come crashing down on him all at once. I had never seen my dad so distraught. I have an uncle who is the spitting imagine of my grandfather, but even so, I believe my dad embodied his father more than any of his brothers. "Family, family, family" was my grandfather's mantra, and he lived it; so, did my dad. My father's crying scared me, and I think I was nine or 10 at the time. After a few days, there were caravans of cars filled with people traveling from California to Arkansas to attend my grandfather's funeral.

The second incident hurtful to my dad, he told me about. I was unaware of the specifics of the incident beforehand and did not realize its impact until my father shared the story with me. In his retelling of the incident, he got choked up and teary eyed. My brother Myron had decided to join the Army. I was in the military. Myron had called my dad at his job to break the news to him. As it happened Myron was leaving that very day. My father took the call; he told me he spoke to Myron, hung up, went into the bathroom at work, just sat there and cried. My dad always had a soft spot for Myron, and the news of my brother hurt him. He certainly wanted Myron to decide his life for himself, but he felt a sadness at Myron's decision to leave rather than him find usefulness at home, either in school or a job.

My dad shared all manner of news, facts, and jokes with me as I got older and our age gap shortened. By the time I was married and had a child, there was no end to the things he'd say to me. I was like, "Whoa, cowboy! There are boundaries, Dad, just chill."

The third incident was directly connected to me. After spending six years in the military serving active duty, three of those years in Germany, I decided to exit the Army permanently and go home. It had been quite a run. I had missed very significant amounts of time with my family. I was still very young, barely 25 at the time, but I had already missed my younger brother's high school years, my sister was entering middle school, and the family had a new family pet, Pepper, a German Shepherd who derived great joy from tearing your ass in half if you bothered any member of the family. I had spent enough time away, and I needed to reconnect with my family.

There was something nobody knew; a secret of sorts that I kept hidden. I was ill-very. My illness forced itself upon me and sapped from me every ounce of energy and life I had in me. I lost the ability to recognize normalcy, and I fought in my head to hold on to some semblance of what I knew to be rational, but to no avail. I was battered daily by the disease, but I was able to put on a smile and pretend to be okay. I wasn't. I was the farthest thing from okay. I was having a difficult transition, and difficult is a euphemism for how I was fairing. I was suffering from a very grave bout of depression that cast a cloud over my entire life for a very long time.

Depression is an awful disease. Its tentacles extend like those of an octopus and slowly wrap around your entire being. The world as you knew it before the depression becomes unrecognizable. You know this, because the tiny bit of rational thought that remains in you tries to get you back to ground zero, the place, the reality where you used to live. Even the smallest of things seems confusing to you. Original thoughts are a lost commodity. You haven't an original thought anymore, because they're all eaten up in the disease. You try to hide yourself from the world, because you're sure everyone knows you're not well and you suspect everyone is talking about the disease and you. These are but some of the basic symptoms. It is part of the confusion caused by the depression. Try as you may, you can no longer make sense of anything, not even yourself. If you have any cognitive function at all, you voluntarily shut yourself off from the world, because you can no longer make sense of it. In some instances, you become paranoid. Every noise, every sound, every utterance has something to do with you. You cannot make sense of simple relationships anymore. The tentacles squeeze off your ability to think and rationalize the world around you. You withdraw. You forget to eat, and you're afraid of everything and everybody, but self-preservation is the first law of nature, and so you put on a face. Every appearance in public is frightening.

I had no idea that I could have non-functioning brain synapses or whatever mumbo jumbo I was being told in my therapy sessions. What also began happening were changed sounds; for example, doors closing, people walking on hardwood floors, and glass shattering were all felt inside my body. With depression your mind has allowed the disease to manifest as a physical ailment. Your whole being, your entire body, hurts, and your mind fails you and continues to get further and further away. Thoughts of uselessness come often. In some instances, neither rare nor extreme, you are unable to work or hold a steady job. At times, you are unable to interact with others on any real or personal level. Your life is a series of moments pretending to be okay when in fact you aren't anything close to okay. In desperation, you begin to think about killing yourself. You need an escape from the pain and the confusion and the failings of your mind and body. The thought of intervention, by doctors or priests is not within your grasp; somebody must lead you to it. Someone near you, who knows you, who is perceptive enough to know things aren't okay, has to decide for you, think for you, and must act with expediency, or you will find a way to kill yourself. Depression is a killer of mind, body, and spirit.

Thank God for my family, and thank God for my friends. Everyone eventually knew I was sick. The most embarrassing part of it all was that it wasn't a secret. I wish it had been. Friends came to visit me (bless them), and I sat and shared with them, but all I wanted was to be left alone. I felt like an exhibit in a circus. But my friends were kind and generous with their time, words, and encouragement. I felt bad, mostly for my parents, who had to take care of me in this condition. To my siblings who held me up high as their older brother, I was like a new born baby, unable to do even the basics.

My dad cried about my situation. He used to like me to watch television with him in the evenings, and I would. We'd start with the news and then watch every program he and my mom liked, up to the 11:00 p.m. news, although my mom would go to bed long before my dad and I finished watching television for the night. It was the love of my parents and the rest of my family that helped me back to sanity.

The details of how I became depressed are not necessary, but I had severe anguish every single day of the experience. I attempted to take my life at least twice. Maybe there was a third attempt, but I don't remember. Each time, there was an intervention. I can only say I am forever thankful to God today for those unplanned interventions. I see now that he had other plans for my life.

I decided it would be best for me to give up recreational highs and all forms of drug use. I found that my body could no longer process the effects of what I had been doing. On a couple occasions, it was funny; I knew internally that it was becoming too corrosive for me. I did not lament quitting. I'd been getting high for most of my teenage and young adult life. It was time to move on. I had thrown away many years in a dead-end pursuit of mind alteration, when I hadn't realized the potency of my own natural state of being. Turning up, as they say, had really been turning down. There wasn't a high out there that I did not try at least once, and most of the time, more than once. It's a blessing today to not only be able to wake up, but also to wake up in my right mind, as the older generation used to say. I gave up narcotics for sobriety, and I've never regretted a day since. But I do have one regret regarding my illness. I was scheduled to be in my cousin Morris's wedding. He and I were like brothers, and always had been. I was too ill to be in the wedding and too embarrassed about my illness to discuss it. To this day, we have never discussed it, and I remain ashamed and embarrassed because of it.

National Pastime

My dad grew up playing baseball, as did most of the men my dad's age, especially black men. At the time they were growing up, baseball was the national pastime, and neither football nor basketball enjoyed the kind of support and participation given to baseball. My dad made sure my brothers and I got involved in playing baseball. We all played little league. Myron and I did not advance beyond that but Greg went on to play professional minor league baseball for an organization. He's the youngest son in the family, 5.5 years younger than Myron and 7.5 years younger than me. But Greg must have hit a growth spurt at some point early on because he grew to be 6'3", while I'm 6'0" and Myron is 5'10" if that.

Baseball enjoyed the lofty place in black culture now given to basketball. We'd go to the barber shop and all talk was about baseball. The men in the shops could quote the stats of their favorite players as easily as someone talking about LeBron, Kobe, or Steph today. And there'd be arguments as to who was the better player, Mays or Aaron, or who you'd rather have pitching in a do or die situation, Koufax or Gibson. Man, that was tough because Koufax had everything-a heater and a monster of a curve-but Gibson threw harder than any pitcher at that time, and he could be formidable if anyone dared try rushing him on the mound.

If he hit someone with a pitch and if they even thought about charging the mound, he would drop his glove and whoop their ass. We grew up in that culture-baseball, baseball, baseball.

Recognition

One-day, years after my father passed away, I was visiting my mom, and she asked me to go to the local supermarket and pick up a few things for her. I did. When I went to the cashier to check out, standing in line in front of me was an older gentleman, a small wiry man who would have been older than my dad had he still been living. The gentleman looked like someone I knew or had met before. I studied him carefully before saying anything, and before he left the cashier, I said, "Amie?" The man turned around and looked at me. I said, "I'm Kenny McClain, Lovie's son." The man came toward me, and within seconds, he recognized me. He held my hand and began to tell me how much he missed my dad, and that he was sorry he did not go to the funeral. He had been away in Israel when he found out my dad had passed away. He asked me to convey this message to my mother. Amie and my dad worked together at Utility Metal Aircraft, a small vendor shop, supplying aircraft parts to the aerospace industry. Amie and my dad were both skilled machinists and worked together for years. Amie's acknowledgement of my dad made me feel good. In the minutes immediately after speaking with Amie, I began thinking about my dad and remembering all that he had exhibited to me through his behavior. My dad had friends of every ilk for as long as I could remember. Amie was Jewish, and he and my dad had been friends and had known each other since the early 60s.

Something inside me felt a little better hearing a good word about my dad that day.

Taking an honest look back at my life and what my parents did to insure we had what we needed, I realized their contributions well beyond their meager means. My parents had little, and what they had, they gave to us. Most of my childhood centered on me, my two brothers, my parents, and later my sister, although she was a late but welcomed and loved addition to our family. We lived in a beautiful middle-class neighborhood where the homes had carefully manicured lawns, were well painted, had front yards, back yards, and swimming pools, and were occupied by families. We got new school clothes at the beginning of each year, and then again midway through the school year. We took family vacations, and every other year, from when I was eight to 17, we caught a train from Pasadena, to Chicago, Illinois, got picked up in Chicago, and drove from there to Milwaukee, Wisconsin. Every other year, five people on the train! When we weren't going to Milwaukee, we were hosting my mom's family at our house for the summer. One year, we deviated from our trip to Milwaukee and drove the family car from Pasadena to Arkansas to visit my dad's mom and my step-grandfather. My paternal grandfather had died years earlier, and my grandmother had remarried.

I am the oldest grandchild on my mother's side of the family. My mom had four sisters, and so far, two of my aunts have passed: Annie and Vicky. My mom is the eldest. Whenever we went to Milwaukee when my grandfather was still alive, he always took me with him someplace and allowed me to go wild without restrictions. My grandfather was a huge man with skin black as coal. It was funny to see him with my grandmother, who was very light skinned, with beautiful gray-green eyes, high cheekbones (some Indian heritage), and petite. You can see an even mix of both my grandparents in my mom.

When I left the house with my grandfather, my grandmother would issue a warning to him she'd say, "Earle, don't do anything stupid with that boy!" My grandfather would say, "C'mon grandson, let's go." We always jumped into the car together and headed off down the street. As soon as we were out of sight of the house, he pulled the car over to the curb and asked if I wanted to drive. Most of the time I'd say no, but I did say yes a couple of times, and he moved over to the passenger seat and allow me to drive as he helped steer the car from the passenger seat.

Driving to Arkansas was an experience. It seemed like we were on the road forever and that we'd never get there. I woke up in the car in the middle of the night one time and I was terrified. Everyone in the car was asleep, and it appeared the car was moving. I started yelling at the top of my lungs. My parents woke up and assured me the car was still, and I was just dreaming. We had arrived at my grandmother's house in the middle of the night, but my parents decided to stay in the car rather than wake my grandmother and her husband in the wee hours of the morning. My grandmother and her husband, Reverend Richardson, were expecting us, so when morning finally did come, they found us outside huddled up in the car. My grandmother married her second husband a couple years after the passing of my paternal grandfather. They lived on a farm complete with animals and the whole lot. There were chickens, pigs, a couple of horse and a cow or three. There was also a pond down the road full of fish, and my grandmother took me and Myron fishing a few times during our visit. There were berry bushes, and I remember a black berry bush in particular. The berries were ripe and very sweet. Myron and I raided the berry bush every day. We tormented the farm animals, too. After all, country life on a farm was foreign to us, and so we chased after the chickens, threw stuff at the pigs, and generally acted foolish out there. My grandmother had one neighbor a short distance from where they lived. The neighbors had a son. He was a couple years older than me, and he was happy to see Myron and me and went out of his way to hang out with us during most of our visit. I believe we stayed a week in Arkansas before making the torturous drive back to California.

My father had a love of politics, but he wasn't overly political; politics weren't something he discussed at length, or at least, I didn't hear them being routinely discussed. However, I did hear, now and again, comments about the big things. Ours wasn't a house with big political debates. I think most of the political banter I heard between my mom and dad was mostly re-hashing something seen on the evening news. The times when politics were discussed in great detail and passion most often occurred when my Uncle George came over and he and my dad debated some political point. My uncle George was my dad's brother in law; he was married to my Aunt Myrlean (dad's oldest sister) and came by often to get my dad riled up about a great many things. Dad loved Uncle George as much as he loved his own flesh and blood brothers. Plus, when Uncle George always came by the house to visit, he always had a conversation of some sort. My dad often felt as though George would save up the most controversial topics to debate with him. I could usually hear my mother in the background laughing at everything that came out of my uncle's mouth.

Awakening

I've seen divisions in America. I've seen the times people took up sides. I've also seen and experienced the growing pains of a nation trying to find itself, and its foundations. I've shared some of the most profound experiences in American History with my parents and, specifically, my father. I don't know why, but I enjoyed watching the news with my dad. He always spoke to me about what we watched from a fully informed perspective. It did not matter whether it was local or national; we always watched the news together. My childhood was filled with some of the most pivotal moments in American history.

The events shaping the nation at the time of my youth were; Vietnam; the assassinations of President John F. Kennedy, Medgar Evers, Malcolm X, Dr. Martin Luther King Jr., and Robert F. Kennedy, and the attempted assassination of Governor George Wallace. We in the Black community witnessed with shame and disgust the first black student trying, and succeeding at gaining entrance to Mississippi State University. There was again shame, outrage, and disgust at the nation and the government for the tepid response to the 16th Street Baptist Church bombing in Birmingham, during which four young black girls lost their lives while attending Sunday church services. We endured during the civil rights march from Selma to Montgomery as well as the Los Angeles Watts riots. I grew up during the first ever televised presidential debate between Nixon and Kennedy. John F. Kennedy was elected president during my youth, and I also saw history made with the moon landing and the walk on the moon by Astronaut Neil Armstrong. All these incredible and pivotal events took place during my youth.

These events thrust the nation into thought and action, or mostly reaction, as there were many voices resisting change in America in the late 60s.

The news anchor was akin to God during those days. The heavy weights were Cronkite, Huntley, Brinkley, Rather, and Wallace. Later came Jenkins and Brokaw. They spoke; we watched.

As I said earlier, my parents cared about the state of the country and cared deeply about the leaders in government, but they were not overly political in their individual personalities. I care about politics- all of it. It does not matter to me whether you are talking about politics in school, work, or government. I realize the potency of being political. The inherent value in understanding politics can come in an up-close and personal observation of human behavior when you least expect it. I heard a statement when I was 13, in junior high, and it went like this: "Stand for something, or you'll fall for anything."

In my opinion, the 45th President of the United States of America is ill fit for the job. He is a bully. Truth is truth. There does not appear to be one person in his inner or outer circle who can or will say or do anything to persuade him to communicate his displeasures in ways other than pointing fingers, avoiding accountability, and acting out and tweeting incessantly like a child. I thought we in America were supposed to go to the voting polls to elect leaders who have sworn to serve the citizens of the country. It appears my thinking is way off. The leaders within his party, the Republican Party, and those who occupy lofty positions within the U.S. Senate and the House of Representatives, have all chosen to close their eyes and ears to his shenanigans and do nothing-a big, fat nothing. The reason is, they have all have been bullied by him and are afraid of him.

The president has made life in America more dangerous for me. He has encouraged racist behaviors with his bullhorn praising fringe (racist) sectors of America. He has done nothing positive to address or to speak out against overly aggressive law enforcement in urban neighborhoods. In addition, his conduct is below the bar of acting presidential. He acts out, like a petulant child in his personal tweet attacks on private citizens. If we are to believe the fantasies peddled out of his administration, he fights, and, as the story goes, he punches back one thousand times harder than those he is punching. Yeah, right-he's a guy who ducked military service because of supposed bone spurs, and a coward who ridiculed a senator within his own political party, a war hero, captured and held as a POW for five years. Nonetheless, we are to believe he punches back one thousand times harder. On his best day, my bet is that he could not punch his way out of a fruit fight. However, being the man, he is, he can "grab a woman by her genitalia and boast about it while also boasting about being able to get away with it." He can also "refuse the norms associated with his office" (revealing tax returns, observing emoluments clauses, and more). And he can even dismiss numerous women who have alleged misconduct with them by him. He can dismiss intelligence reports telling him a foreign country, an adversary, has attacked our democracy, and ignore the intelligence in favor of giving cover to the adversary. There is something wrong with this picture.

This president has made bullying his character of choice. It is a failed character choice and is markedly different than, say, one who acts or becomes assertive as a way to defend themselves. I am in agreement with self-protecting. I think I would do whatever necessary to protect myself and my loved ones if I felt or thought someone were trying to do me or my loved one's harm. And, I am also aware of harm's many different forms, i.e., physical, mental, emotional, and financial, to name a few. But I cannot remember another instance in which a U.S. president felt the need to act against an American citizen in a public forum or to go after foreign allies and the U.S. Press Corps. It's not only sheer madness, but also straight up bully behavior.

In the society in which I live, in the United States of America, the life of a black man is not valued as equal to the life of a white man. The amount of success one has achieved doesn't matter, if you're black your legitimacy will at some point be called into question. This never happens when you are white. You are legitimate simply because you are Caucasian. We needn't consult a sociologist for this fact. Further, black men are tagged with the stereotypes of angry, dangerous, and hostile, which puts a bullseye on us every time we step outside the protection of our homes. Black families have to worry whether their son, daughter, aunt, uncle, brother, sister, mom, or dad will come home safely at the end of the night, or whether the phone will ring, and they'll be told go to the hospital or the police station, or even the morgue. Black men in particular are expected to be docile, never or protective of themselves or their families, and when we are upset enough to express ourselves, we put ourselves in danger of being killed by either the police or a random citizen, citing a stand-your-ground defense. Let that sink in. Yet, I don't know of anyone, not one single person, who, when they hear about a mass shooting anywhere in America, first think of a black man.

Mass shootings are occurring with more frequency and intensity, and nobody and no place is safe. They are happening at schools, synagogues, churches, night clubs, movie theatre, shopping centers, concerts, and work spaces, and everywhere else. Who do come to mind, almost immediately, in every instance of the aforementioned tragedies, are white men between the ages of 15 and 50. I'm not saying we paint all Caucasian males as dangerous, but there is a pattern of such men doing mass shootings in America.

These crimes are committed, and neither the government nor the press will call them what they are: terrorist acts. The government and the press use all kinds of word salad to downplay this fact and instead refer to such acts as simply as gun violence.

However, American society expects me, a black man, in all instances of confrontation, to hold my tongue, defuse my anger, and remember political correctness. It has gotten to the point that when confronted with adverse situations and direct confrontation, people just do not care anymore. I have observed in people an, "I give zero fucks" attitude. In some respects, it can be refreshing. In other respects, limiting. Personally, I have always been passionate about the causes near and dear to me, and it is a personal challenge for me to be reserved or detached from that passion.

Nevertheless, as my guide post, my dad was always someone I could check in with to temper my passion, and he was intuitive enough to often pick up on anything unsettling in my life without me needing to say anything. I am constantly at work on tempering my personal volcanic energy, but I do feel it necessary at times to display my passion. I cannot pretend anymore to be blind to the injustices still taking place in America. I am a black man for God's sake, I cannot ignore the ignorance pelted at African American men, women, and children daily in what sometimes feels like a racist America. I do not mean to suggest that all of America is racist, because it isn't, but I am dismayed at how much racism still exists in the country. I'm saddened beyond words that the well of empathy for the less fortunate appears to be empty, for the most part. Why does America ask me to be tolerant, to make sacrifices, to be understanding of the mountain of ignorance and bigotry I face? I cannot unsee what is plainly out in the open. I cannot talk rationally or dispassionately about police officers killing black men in the streets, and in their cars, homes, apartments, and backyards in cities all over America. Yet I must wait with baited breath to hear an explanation as to why these events occur. What we end up getting is a press briefing on how the shootings, and other acts of terrorism have been investigated and determined to be justified. What independent panel is doing these investigations?

No, I cannot un-see innocent black people having the police called on them simply because they take a seat in a coffee shop or work out in a gym. Black families are pushed to the brink by these killings and unfair practices, which continue to happen with alarming rates of reoccurrence. Oh, America, where is your shining light? Why do you further crush us and refuse to punish those who have committed crimes against us, even when some wear the protector's uniform, knowing they deserve to answer for the crimes they have committed? There have been outright murders committed for which the perpetrators have walked away scot-free.

I cannot temper my disgust at the blatant and open bigotry that was spewed at the first African American President of the United States, as well as First Family while the president was in office. I do not want to be, nor am I, the black office guy who is so cool I laugh along with the racial jokes about blacks and other minorities because I'm different. No, I am not different. I am for all of humanity, but I will never forget that I am black first.

Colin Kaepernick, a former celebrated quarterback for the San Francisco 49ers professional football team, decided to quietly protest the inequalities in American society, specifically the shooting of unarmed black youth and men. He protested silently by taking a knee during the playing of the National Anthem which is played just before the opening kickoff of each football game. Because he chose to take a stand against these injustices, he was summarily dismissed from his team and blackballed by every football team in the league. Colin has not played football in more than three years yet he remains ready to return to work. This shows collusion on the part of the owners, who have basically said, "Stay in your lane, which is playing football, and do not speak out on social issues." Similarly, celebrated opinion host of a cable news giant even suggested for noted and celebrated NBA basketball star LeBron James, should shut and dribble and not speak about issues outside his paid profession. Let me just say, that that did not go over well. James; one opinion host zero.

I would be able to discuss these issues, my viewpoints, and next steps with my dad if he were around. As a father I do all that I can to parent my children in a way that will allow them to be educated, responsible contributors to the betterment of America. My children are respectful, earnest, loyal, and proud of who they are and where they come from. So why is a different set of scales used when judging my kids than when judging others who are different from them only in appearance? Their hue should not determine their worth.

On Notice

My father's health had been in a slow decline for years prior to his death. There was an unexpected diagnosis of renal failure and a need for dialysis. The root cause of the renal failure was hypertension. The doctor reasoned my dad had gone years without the proper medical protocols for a man his age. If he had gone for regular medical checkups, he would have known about his high blood pressure long before it turned into his nightmare of ruined kidneys. The damage to his kidneys was a direct result of the neglect.

However, putting a focus on the entirety of his life can show you there were other, earlier ailments as well. During the early years of my childhood, my father was over-weight and he remained so for a long time. He stood 5'9", and I guess he weighed as much as 230 lbs. or more at his heaviest. His weight gains and the fact that he remained heavy could be attributed to his love of food - soul food, junk food, fast food, and most anything else ending in "food". My dad was mostly a "see food" eater. He ate everything in his line of vision. The presence of food at home and the places he frequented, combined with his voracious appetite, was a recipe for disaster. My dad was a Southerner, and given the times in which he grew up, I imagine he grew up with a diet that consisted of foods high in fatty products, including saturated fats, and sweets, carbs, and starches.

His Mom, my grandmother was a good cook and my mother was (and is) a good cook. My mom, hailing from the South could cook all the foods my dad liked. A typical dinner at my house would usually consists of meat, a starch, a vegetable, and something to drink, more often than not sweetened with sugar. So, on any given night, a meal could be meat loaf, mashed potatoes or rice with butter and sugar, mixed vegetables, and bread or biscuits; the helpings were huge. And as I said, it was all washed down with Kool-Aid or iced tea loaded up with sugar. I remember that years later, when I was a grown man, I was invited to a friend's house for dinner. The family was Asian, and I knew them well. Dinner was served, and rice was one of the staples. I recall asking for butter and sugar for my rice. I thought everyone at the table was going to lose a rib laughing so hard. They thought that surely, I had lost my mind. I did not know of any other way to eat rice than to add butter and sugar.

What else is known about my family's dietary leanings is that we ate desserts. This is where I once again compliment my mom, because her skills in the kitchen extended to baking. My mom had definite "grand slam" baking moments. Her sweet potato pies, coconut cakes, and German chocolate cakes were hits. But there wasn't just food in our house; there was also food at extended family's houses. If my dad visited either of his sisters, my aunts Myrlean and Mae, there'd be food at their houses as well-lots of it and plenty of it delicious.

My dad resembled a man who delighted in eating. He was funny, too, because as fat as he was at times, he did not seem to care. He walked around the house with his shirt off on occasion, and his big belly stuck out as if he had swallowed a watermelon. I thought, "Man, that thing looks painful." I joked every now and then about his fat stomach, and he'd just laugh and said, "Go on, boy; get outta my way."

I joined the U.S. Army at age 19. I had just finished a year attending my city's college and the truth was I was not a very good student at the time. I knew that I had to do something, so I enlisted in the Army, thinking that for the time being, my service would be an adequate substitute for college. When I joined there happened to be, among the young black soldiers, a very pro-conscious, pro-black, progressive movement within the military structure. One of the "no-no's" of this was eating of pork. And so, being in the group I stopped. The first visit I had home for a family dinner, I announced to my parents my renouncing of pork. I was certain my parents wouldn't understand, but what I found was that my parents were completely supportive of my decision. A conversation was had between my mom and dad, and afterward my mom started seasoning food with smoked turkey rather than pork. It was nice to be able to eat my mom's cooking and not worry if there was pork in the pot. She did not stop cooking with pork altogether because it was such a staple in our house, but she did cut way back on it and there was always another option if I was at home.

The aircraft parts business for local and small vendors began to shrink and people lost their jobs in the early 80s. Many jobs simply went away, and the jobs that did not were folded into whatever larger corporations took over smaller shops. This loss of jobs left a huge void for my dad and many of his friends, who had worked most of their lives in the industry. My guess is that my dad, by that time had spent nearly 30 years working in the aircraft parts business. When the jobs went away, my dad was out of work for what seemed like a long time. There weren't a lot of skills that could be transferred from being a precision aircraft parts machinist into something else. Luckily, my mom had a well-paying job in the education sector, and it sustained things. I was long gone from my parents' house by this time. My dad's job search was long and difficult, but eventually, he found a job working at the Beverly Center, a big brand new big mall in West LA. The job was menial, but it was something he could go to every day, receive a paycheck, and contribute to the household to feel good about himself.

Our family, for as long as I can remember, had two cars. When my dad found his new job, he decided he'd take public transportation to and from work. The decision was a good one on a couple levels. First, he had to do a fair amount of walking to and from bus stops, and there was a fair amount of walking associated with his job. Second, because he walked a lot, he dropped a lot of weight, I'd guess 60 lbs., over 18 months. The transformation was a big one. Dad had already quit smoking cigarettes before he'd gotten the new job, and with the weight loss, things were looking up for him.

However, my father caught a cold that refused to go away and just lingered. It held on and never let him go. He knew that beating the cold would be easy if he opted out of work for a couple days and just stayed home to rest. But knowing a thing and practicing a thing is where you find the gaps. He did not stay home from work, and the cold did not go away.

Dad was at work one day, still feeling the effects of that cold, when he happened upon his supervisor, a young white guy not much older than I was. I say this based on the description I received from my dad. He and my father forged a friendly relationship, and, according to my dad, they talked about everything, although mostly sports. He saw my dad that morning and was immediately concerned with his appearance. After an initial conversation, he told my dad that he wanted him to leave work, go home, see a doctor, and not return to work without a doctor's note.

This instruction, according to my dad, was a bit much, even coming from someone he liked and considered a friend. It's one thing for someone to show concern, but it was another for that young guy to tell my dad he wouldn't be allowed back to work unless he could produce a doctor's note. This put my dad in a pinch. He wasn't in the habit of making doctor visits unless absolutely necessary, and for minor things, he self-diagnosed rather than go to a doctor. But, he'd been told by his supervisor that unless he could produce a note, he would not be allowed back on the job. He left work and took a bus home, but stopped at urgent care clinic so he could see a doctor. While there he described the cold, how long he'd had it, and other symptoms he was having at the time. They did all the requisite things one would get in an office visit, including drawing blood. After the visit, he took the bus home. The doctor had suggested that he stay home from work for a couple days. I was unaware of any of this at the time, other than my mom mentioning that my dad had a cold and was home from work.

The next day, I worked half a shift at my own job. I decided to use the second half of the day to drive over to my parents' house to hang out with my dad. When I got there, my dad was surprised and happy to see me. He offered me some lunch, we talked and then we began watching Phil Donahue. The phone rang and dad got up to answer the phone. We were in the den at the time, and the nearest phone was a rotary phone that hung on the kitchen wall. Dad stood in the doorway between the den and the kitchen as he spoke. I stayed seated and continued to watch the show, but during his conversation, heard him say, "Yes," "No'" "Okay," "When," "Okay," He hung the phone up and asked me if I had anything pressing to do, and I said, "No." He explained that the call was from the clinic, and while calling on a few people who had blood drawn from the day before, someone's blood showed an ill composition. The clinic was asking a few of the patients to return to the hospital to have blood drawn a second time. So, he asked me if I had time to take him over to the hospital to have his blood drawn. They promised to do an analysis on the spot if we went right over. I said "Yes," he got dressed and we drove 25-30 minutes to get the test done.

We arrived and he checked in, and in no time his name was called to go to the lab to have his blood drawn. I went with him. Once the blood was drawn, we went to a waiting room. After a brief interval, they called his name, and he disappeared into a doctor's office. I stayed seated in the waiting room with a magazine. The time was around 3:30 p.m. First, 25 minutes went by, then 40 minutes, one hour, 90 minutes, and two hours, and I was really concerned as no one had said anything to me. After more than two hours I finally got up to see what the issue was and at the same time, the hospital rolled my father out of the doctor's offices in a wheelchair. He had a smile on his face, but I could tell he was scared. I thought "WTF?" He just went in to have blood drawn; why is he in a wheel chair? I was totally confused. He told me not to worry, but to get my mom and bring her back to the hospital. His blood sample showed his body was in renal failure.

There were two options; a kidney transplant or dialysis, for which he would go to the hospital a minimum of three times a week to have his blood cleaned.

He was going to have to start dialysis immediately, even if he wanted a transplant. Further, he was going to have to make lifestyle changes immediately as well. The whole thing took my entire family by shock. As I said before, my dad was strong, proud, and courageous, but he was going to have a battle like none he had never faced before. I knew my dad well enough to know that in that instance, he was afraid. It was a challenge that he couldn't outsmart, or beat into submission. His body was in a state of decline, such that it was going to take all the modern miracles of medicine to put him back together. The hypertension had engulfed his body entirely, and he was completely unaware, hence the nickname for hypertension, the silent killer. I asked him if he had experienced any symptoms at all, or had any inkling that he was ill. He remembered that when going to urinate, it would take some time before his stream began. One indicator that you might need your kidneys checked is if you have a delay in your water stream when you go to urinate. It is supposedly one of the tell-tale signs in men.

I hated that new chapter in my dad's life, but to his credit, he embraced the challenge and followed his doctor's orders fully.

My dad's supervisor was a hero of sorts, and here's the why of it: there was a reason that young man had been adamant that Dad see a doctor and not return to work until he had a doctor's note. That young man was the primary care taker for his mother, who also had renal failure. He had been taking care of his mom long enough to recognize some of the signs of distress in the body. In being attentive to his own mother, one of the things he noted was the whiteness of her eyes. He noticed the same whiteness in my dad's eyes that morning. My dad started their conversation saying he felt under the weather. The supervisor sensed something more than just a cold in my dad. On some level, he saved my dad's life. The doctors told us, that the first night my dad was in the hospital, his blood pressure was so high he could have had a devastating stroke at any time. He was lucky to be up and walking around.

Dad had to undergo an emergency surgery to put a shunt in his body to begin the dialysis treatment. The first surgery was to install a temporary shunt, and then there would be a surgery during which a permanent shunt would be placed in his wrist. In his initial surgery, they placed the shunt in the left side of his neck. Oh, Jesus, I wanted to cry. It was then that I began to see my dad in a whole new light. His tenderness bled through the façade of hardness he held onto raising 3 sons and one daughter. He was vulnerable. I wanted desperately for it to be all a dream and for my dad to go back to the person I knew him to be as before the illness. I was devastated; we all were. The new and challenging diagnosis, needing dialysis three times a week, and the need for an entire lifestyle change affected not only his physical body, but also, his entire being.

I remember Cindie, my ex-wife, and I were in the car driving someplace. I don't remember exactly where we going, but I do remember we were on a freeway heading south. My dad had just begun his medical journey, the beginning of his dialysis treatments. Cindie turned to me in the car and said, "The life span of patients who under-go dialysis is about six years after the start of treatment." That statement triggered an argument between us. What Cindie was trying to tell me, I did not want to hear; I didn't ask for the information, and she did not have to give it to me. The words, for me, were very hurtful. But Cindie was a nurse, and to her credit, she wanted me to be educated on what all of it meant. Cindie wasn't one to bury her head in the sand. Nurses deal with medical challenges in patients all the time, and at times, their speech reflects their vocation. Cindie's mother had been a nurse as well. The medical community speaks on medical matters as routinely as a barber speaks about good and bad haircuts.

Once my dad started dialysis, he continued until the day of his passing. And he passed away roughly six years after the start of the treatment. He got up at 4:00 a.m. three days a week to get over to the hospital to sit for the three hour treatment. God bless whoever invented that dialysis machine, and God bless the medical people who treated my dad. He was very likeable, and by the time he was a regular at the treatment center, he was a favorite patient. I went over to the hospital once, to sit with him while he received his treatment. I remember it was surprising for him that I showed up. He was happy to see me, and the hospital staff allowed me to go in and sit right beside him the whole time. We talked about everything that day. I was glad that I went, because I saw the treatment and could better understand better what patients went through.

One very painful thought for me today is why I didn't offer to give my dad one of my good kidneys. I believe, had we thought outside the box even a tiny bit, either me or one of my brothers would have gladly given my dad a kidney. I don't know why this wasn't explored as an option. I ask myself this question, but in the end, I know my father would have said, no anyway. He was, on some level, proud and stubborn. He would have believed he was stripping us of our wholeness, and possibly putting our lives in jeopardy, if we had agreed to donate a kidney.

Here we go

My friend Tony Thomas and I were smoking weed one night, as getting high was our usual form of recreation. In an instant, we went from being high and not caring about anything to sheer panic and anxiety when, out of nowhere, my dad walked up on us. To understand the magnitude of fear, that gripped us in that moment, you have to know my dad for all that he was and could be.

Lovie McClain, my pops, was no joke. He could be a strict disciplinarian, and was, when necessary. He had a serious side that, when expressed, was arguably one of the scariest someone could encounter. His voice was a deep rich baritone that could be intimidating even in its resting state. His frame of reference for doling out discipline came from a variety of places: His service in the Korean conflict; growing up in the south; segregation; Jim Crow; and the additional oppressive conditions African Americans were made to face during the 30s, 40s, and 50s, in the South, essentially the early years of his life. My father used to say to me, "I feel sorry for you, boy." Initially when he said that to me, I didn't know exactly what he meant, but he did explain to me later. He felt that growing up in the segregated south, the language of separation and segregation was very easy to understand, because it was made plain, that if you were colored, you lived in one place, and Whites lived in another. He felt for us, in that he believed we were growing up without any real understanding of what racism is and how it can tear apart a country and its citizens. We were his kids, but born, and raised, in California. My father believed California to be just as toxic as the South, but also believed that the state did a better job masking its prejudices.

He was a proud man, maybe even prideful. He felt this way because he was self-made, and aside from high school, he was self-educated. My dad was also very self-aware. He understood the power of education and communication in all forms, and although he had only high school as his formal education, he never stopped learning. As I mentioned before he was a skilled machinist who worked in the aerospace industry manufacturing precision aircraft parts for several aerospace and commercial defense companies. He was affable with friends everywhere, long before anyone thought or said it was cool to have friends of varying ethnicities, and he was also a devoted husband, father, brother, uncle, son, neighbor, and man of the world. His parenting style was liberal, yet guiding, and as I said earlier, he had my mom's back whenever she felt she needed a heavy hand to guide us or strike the fear of God in us. His no nonsense approach worked.

There is one thing about my dad that made me laugh out loud. He started wearing glasses at around age 50. He made no fuss about the fact. He went out and bought black-wide framed glasses, which made him, look like a big geek. My mom hated him wearing those glasses, and she tried to make him leave the glasses at home whenever they went out to social functions. My dad had zero cares in the world about how others saw him. He wore the glasses proudly and, more importantly, because he needed them to see. His retort was "I don't give a damn," and he didn't.

So, when Tony and I sat in my car that fateful night, smoking weed, listening to Marvin Gaye, and whatever else we were listening to, we were naïve regarding the fate that awaited us, and we were deaf to the fact that we were blaring music into the night at 12:30 a.m. My father had come outside to tell us to turn down the music so we wouldn't wake the neighbors. He had no idea what we were doing.

The windows were fogged up like a mutha with smoke from the weed. You know how it is when you're smoking and you want to keep the smoke in to continue the contact high. By mere accident, Tony noticed movement: opening the gate to the driveway from the patio opening. Whoever was there was making their way toward the car. We were parked in a lower part of the driveway, adjacent to my house. My parents' and the neighbor had a shared driveway, that divided once you entered the upper portion of the driveway. As you went further up, each home-owner had their own driveway space just outside their house. My car was parked just outside our garage, behind our second car, essentially outside my parents' and neighbors' bedroom windows.

So, we were sitting there grooving to the music, and then suddenly, Tony was saying, "Here comes Lovie-oh shit! We had that single; oh shit!" We thought in unison, "Oh Shit!! He could, if he wanted, bring the wrath of God." We were certain he was about to rain ass whooping on both of us.

He tapped on the window, and said, "Kenneth roll down the window." I sat there frozen, pretty much in a stupor, or rather like dazed and confused, from the weed and scared that I was about to be sent to meet Jesus. He said again, only a little more aggressively, "Kenneth, roll down the window." As I did, the smoke just poured out the window into his nostrils. It was like I was watching it in slow motion. It was like a cartoon, and it was actually funny to watch. He staggered backwards from the car, as if to say," WTF Kenny!" But he was cool and told us to turn down the music, as he stressed his concern that the music might wake Mr. and Mrs. Rodgers, the neighbors. To my dad's credit, and to my and Tony's complete surprise, he never mentioned that incident to me. I doubt he said anything to my mother about it, either. As a matter of fact,

I know he didn't, because had he done that, he would have had to explain why he had chosen to do nothing rather than to punish us.

My dad liked Tony. As a matter of fact, he liked all my close friends at the time: Tony, Stan, Richard, Jerome, Jack, and Freddy. That was my clique that had the privilege, if they decided to exercise it, to call my dad by his first name, Lovie. He thought it was funny. But my friends all grew up in respectful households, so no one dared call my dad by his first name. They all called him Mr. McClain, and rightly so.

In retrospect, I should not have been doing what I was doing that night. I say that because I shared a bedroom with my two younger brothers, and they probably smelled the weed on me when I went into the room. I haven't a clue what I was thinking back then, and when I do think about it now, it's plain to me that I wasn't thinking at all.

As I said before, my mom and dad met in the Midwest, but the funny thing they were originally both from the South. My mom was born in Mississippi and lived there until around age 11. My grandfather wanted out of the South and so-he moved his family up from there to the Midwest. My dad was born in the South and stayed there through high school. He left the summer after he graduated to visit a cousin who lived in the Midwest. He had plans to enter the military, as well. It was during that visit with the cousin that he met my mom. Not long after that he had to leave for military duty.

In a very short period of time after joining the Marines, he was fighting in the war in South Korea, or the Korean conflict as it is known today. My father was wounded in the war. I learned of his injury when I was very young. I saw my dad working in the back-yard or doing some work around the house, and sometimes he was shirtless. I was drawn to an almost deformed area on his right shoulder that went around to the upper most part of his back on his right side. The area had large bumps around it, not quite keloid, but I knew something had occurred. Myron and I would ask about it all the time. Finally, one day, we got an answer. He said that during the conflict, he and his team came under heavy enemy fire. They were hunkered down in a fox hole trying to wait it out. One of the guys with him said, "Mac, I'm going to make a run for it." My dad said he told the guy not to do it because of the incoming fire and shells directed at them. At some point, the guy panicked and ran anyway. My dad said that within seconds, the guy sustained a direct hit and was blown to bits. About this time, my father figured he'd be killed if he stayed, so he dashed out as well. He made it to a safe space, but he rotated his body around, and his whole upper right shoulder split apart. He was hit by shrapnel. He was sewn up in the field, and at the first opportunity, he was airlifted to a hospital in Japan. He stayed there until he became healthy, and then returned to duty in Korea. Hero? Yeah, definitely.

After he was discharged from the Marines, he returned to the Midwest, where he and my mom resumed their relationship. Not long after, they were married. My mom was 19. Their wedding was in her hometown in December 1953. That's a festive month for us, as my mom was born in December, I was born in December, my dad was born in December, and my parents were married in December. As I mentioned before I'm the oldest of five children born to my mom and dad. We came out as four boys and one girl. My youngest brother, who was given the name Gerald at birth, died suddenly as an infant. Gerald's death was devastating for us as a family. I was 9.5 years old at the time and completely unaware of the finality of death. "Death" was not yet a part of my vocabulary, and it wasn't until Gerald died that I understood what it meant.

I was at a loss emotionally because of Gerald's death, although I place no blame whatsoever on my parents, who were also dealing with it. But at 9.5, I was left alone psychologically to deal with the death of my baby brother. The whole family was attached to my mother's pregnancy. We joked about names, the sex of the child, nicknames, and more. My mom's friends and family had given gifts, the house was set up and everything. The only thing we needed was for my mom to have the baby and bring him home. The loss of Gerald was extreme.

While I didn't have any professional help dealing with my grief, neither did my brother Myron, who, I'm sure, suffered too. Greg was only one month from turning two when Gerald died, so he was not processing anything beyond his next meal. I had been so excited when my mom was taken to the hospital to deliver. In those days, women went to the hospital to give birth and normally stayed about three days before returning home. I was expecting my mom to return home in a few days with the new baby. After she gave birth, I knew the baby was a boy and looked like Myron. I ran home the day I knew my mom, dad, and the baby would be home. I was excited, and my heart pumping as I ran up the driveway to the back, where I'd enter the patio and then the back door. I was met by Myron, who, with a blank face, staring directly at me, said very simply, "The baby died."

Myron is chocolatey, a beautiful dark-roast brown complexion with chubby cheeks and a cherub smile. He has always carried a few extra pounds on him. In his early years, he was a spitting image of my dad, stout with a dead pan expression worn purposely on his face.

That day, his face was completely expressionless as he let me know that our brother had died. Poor Myron. He stood there quiet and resolute. The splitting image of my dad and a pillar of strength at seven years old.

What was I meant to do after he made the statement, "The baby died?" My excited 10-year-old brain could not process what he was saying, but he said it again: "The baby died." As I stood there frozen in disbelief, my father came around the corner from his bedroom, and in one motion, hugged me and Myron as if he were squeezing the breath out of us. We all cried. I remember the strength of my father's hug as he explained to me what happened. A generic explanation is that Gerald passed away due to blue baby syndrome known as tetralogy of fallot.

My mother was completely torn apart by Gerald's passing, and I don't remember her coming out of her bedroom for what seemed like months, although it was probably just days.

My dad exhibited Herculean strength during that time of mourning in our house. He still had to get up each day, go to work, and care for my mom and for us three boys at home. For days after our loss, I went to school and just cried all day. I went door to door on my block and retold the story of my brother dying. The neighbors, bless their hearts, took care of me emotionally. I guess they realized how lost I was, and according to "village rules" I was their responsibility as my parents'. I can't say when things went back to being okay, but I'm certain my parents carried the loss of Gerald with them their whole lives. It happened in 1965 but I am still raw when I think about that day.

Pasadena/Altadena, CA

Pasadena, California is gorgeous. Its appeal is that it's an ideal city in which to live and raise a family. It sits in the San Gabriel Valley in a north-eastern part of Los Angeles County, bordered by the San Gabriel Mountains to the north, a short 35-40-minute drive to the shore's edge and beaches to the south, with picture perfect weather year round, a diverse population, and low crime, and it should be listed as one of the most desirable cities to live in all of America. It is home to the Rose Bowl, the Rose Parade, Pasadena City College, Huntington Library, Huntington Hospital, and the finest medical care one can find from various practices. Many great Americans first called Pasadena home, including the legendary athlete and American Jackie Robinson. I say, without hesitation, that I'm proud to be from Pasadena, as its reputation is second to none.

I grew up with great neighbors on either side of me and all up and down my block. When we first moved to Altadena, from a duplex in Pasadena we essentially integrated into a neighborhood where there were already a few African American families and couples. My dad was employed at Utility Metal Aircraft, the huge manufacturing firm that, as I mentioned before provided aircraft parts to defense contractors and some commercial carriers. The firm was being bought out by another firm, and as a part of the buyout, they emptied everyone's retirement account, paid them, and started a new retirement plan. My dad took his money and purchased our home. I remember him telling me the monthly payment was going to be $ 119.00 each month. That was a huge amount of money in 1960, and the purchase price of the house, I believe was $ 39,000.00. At any rate, the price and the payment were dizzying to my dad. But I know my mom, and she pushed him to close the deal. I'm certain that after the fact, he appreciated the loving nudge.

This was a huge move for my parents, who weren't yet out of their 20s, but had two kids. What was also central to this was the fact that they bought in an integrated neighborhood above the "Mason-Dixon line," which divided Pasadena from Altadena. In those days, most everyone had their phone number listed in the yellow pages, but my parents had an unlisted number. It's the same number my mother has today, nearly 60 years later. Well, my father said that the ink wasn't dry on the house papers when he began to receive anonymous phone calls from various voices, saying, "Nigger, you must think you're big shit." My dad said it happened on a regular basis. He finally got used to the calls and stopped answering the phone.

Terrace street, where I grew up, sits on a three- street cul de sac and was slightly racially mixed in 1960. Although as it eventually began to gain more color, the white families took flight and moved either higher up in the foothills, or east to Sierra Madre, Arcadia, or in some cases to east Pasadena.

The family directly across the street from us was Caucasian. With a husband, wife, and three kids. Two of the children one boy and one girl, were older than me, but their youngest son and I were about the same age. The family was cool; since I was five years old when we moved, I'm not exactly sure how they welcomed my parents, but it's clear to me that the welcoming must have been okay, because I cannot remember a time when I did not play with their son; I was always at their house or he was always at mine. In fact, his mom used to pile the neighborhood kids into her car about once every couple weeks, and take us down to Brookside Park. It was just south of the Rose Bowl in Pasadena. She took us there so we could swim in the public pool all day.

Those neighbors did eventually move but I doubt it had anything to do with more African Americans moving into the neighborhood. I think they finally got the price they wanted for their house, and they took the money and bought a bigger house. I remember going to that bigger house higher up in the foothills and playing and playing for hours. They had lots of avocado trees there.

There were also the Humphreys, another Caucasian family on our block, and their son, Tim. He and I played together; it seemed every day. On one of the streets that made up the cul de sac were also the Coooperuds and their son, Barry. He might as well have been black because all he ever did was hang out with us and beat the crap out of anyone in the neighborhood who professed to be able to play basketball. Barry could straight up whoop your ass on the court. He could flat ball, and that is he had a great ability to play basketball.

My brothers and I had a blast growing up. There were the usual expectations; we had chores to do every Saturday before we could play. But our parents, as strict as we thought them to be at the time, were quite liberal. We had outside play privileges for any day and any time we wanted. There were usually no restrictions other than to be in the house by a certain time during school days, and that curfew was much later on the weekends. Now that I'm a parent I know my parents were happy to have us out of the house, and playing so that they could get some relief. My block was filled with kids, boys and girls who all played well together. It was nothing to get a small baseball game going or touch football in the street. When the whole block was down for something at night, we'd play a killer game of hide and seek or hot peas and butter. We made up a game as well, called "pom pom polaway," and it was loads of fun, especially when most of the block played. Hot peas and butter was fun, too, because ultimately you could beat the crap out of someone if you wanted to, under the protection of the game. I did abuse the power a couple times.

As a kid, teenager, and young adult, the demographics of my neighborhood were not a priority, nor were they subject to examination. It appears it didn't matter, though, because the schools I attended were racially mixed, although, as I remember there were more White students than Black students at my schools. Also, as I recall when we initially moved to Altadena, the racial mix was mostly White with some Black and a noticeable absence of Hispanic and Asian residents. The Hispanics came later, but there was never a big influx of Asians. A few came eventually, but they could primarily be found in the northeastern part of the county.

I do remember one Mexican family in particular, the García's. I remember them because I was friends with their two boys, who were my age and no kid or teenager who knew Mrs. Garcia could forget her. She was gorgeous, as fine as any woman alive at the time, and was definitely a must see for any teenage boy going through puberty. Ralph and Dino were two very cool Mexicans. Mr. Garcia was also cool, and he knew i. I can't remember many details about him, other than the fact that he seemed like a hard-working father devoted to his family and, probably, devoted to sexing up Mrs. Garcia every chance available.

I was a bright kid; I really didn't know it at the time, but it is true; I was smarter than most kids my age and grade. I was also gifted with lots of personality. I could read at a level higher than most children in my grade level, and math was a second language to me. I went to public school at a time when public school was just as good as any private school and, in some instances, better. Private schools could not give you the socialization you needed as a part of your fundamental growth. The enrollments were too low. Further, kids going to private schools often felt isolated from the kids in their communities, and when I was in grade school, public schools supplied books and any other materials needed. Field trips were free, or almost free, and there were at least two field trips per grade school year. The teachers were firm; you were to leave your personal stuff, whatever it was, at the door. I didn't know what a parochial school was, but I guarantee you, the teachers where I went to school were just as firm, knowledgeable, and no-nonsense as those teaching in parochial schools. I think teachers could still give spankings. You either learned or you had the teacher leaning on your butt constantly. I learned. I think the only times I got into trouble were when I was goofing around with my friends in class and when I began to believe girls were noticing me. I was around 12 when puberty began.

The early years in school, grades one to six were a breeze for me. I coasted through spelling my name. When it was time to go to junior high known as middle school now grades seven to nine, I realized that I had been put in all accelerated classes. Man, stuff started to zoom; I mean, I had algebra; science, which was not social science; Spanish; and a host of other classes that had I really applied myself, could have led to a spectacular career in something. And I did apply myself at first; I more than held my own and I was quite casual about the fact that I was competing with kids in higher grades in these accelerated classes. When I say elementary was a cake walk, I mean I sliced through those elementary lessons with the greatest of ease. But in junior high, I had to think, and I enjoyed the ability to think and reason with the school's brightest students. I can plainly see now that what I had at that time, my ability to think and reason beyond my classmates, was a unique and special gift.

My 5th grade teacher at Edison Elementary School remains one of the most influential people in my life. I don't believe I'll ever forget her. Her name was Mrs. Almore. She was a black woman, in her 30s, about 5'4" in height, with a plump or chubby build. She had a very cute face and beautiful smooth brown skin. I remember, because in addition to having to look at her in front of the classroom every day, I thought she had unusually big, clear, beautiful brown eyes. And Mrs. Almore recognized something in me. She never said exactly what it was she saw, but whatever it was, it must have remained present, because she was constantly riding me for excellence. She would not let me take one day off to slack. Every day in class, it was "Kenny this," or "Kenny that," indicating her displeasure at me settling or not doing my best. I remember she pitted me in a spelling contest against a guy who was thought to be as smart as me, and he beat me. I remember the word that tripped me up: "accommodation" I spelled it with one "c" instead of two. She sat at her desk and smirked at my loss.

Three years prior to having Mrs. Almore for fifth grade, I had Mrs. Dixon for second grade. One November, we were playing outside during the last morning recess. Suddenly, the school bell starts ringing, ringing, and ringing. The teachers started running out of the buildings onto the playgrounds, rounding up all of the kids, and bringing us back into the classrooms. We knew it wasn't an earthquake drill, but we didn't know what it could be. If it were a real earthquake, we knew we would be able to feel the ground shaking. The teachers, counselors, and everyone who was an adult seemed terribly upset. There appeared to be a lot of confusion, and none of the students had any idea about the source of it. Once we were all accounted for and in our classroom, Mrs. Dixon, crying, announced to us, that the President had been shot. President John F. Kennedy had been shot in Dallas, Texas, and had been taken to the hospital. The school announced that our parents had been called in order for them to come to the school to get us. Any students who regularly walked home were free to leave. I found my little brother, and we walked home with friends. Nobody spoke as we walked. There was none of the usual playfulness that accompanied our daily walks home. I held Myron's hand, and we navigated the three blocks. Mom was there when Myron and I arrived. She was with Greg, who was seven months old, and appeared agitated as she watched the news coverage. In what seemed like a short span of time, the news anchor reported the president was dead.

It was a sad time; the country mourned. My mom and dad were Kennedy supporters, and I suspect most of his supporters were in the African American community. For some reason, John F. Kennedy was thought to be not just the president, but also a great liberator for the African American community.

A correction should be noted here; we weren't African Americans at this time, we were still Negroes. It was a few years later when James Brown's anthem "I'm Black and I'm Proud" changed the thinking and consciousness of Negro America. I remember clearly the day I heard that record. I was in a car on the banks of Lake Michigan in Milwaukee, Wisconsin when James Brown came blaring through the window, shouting, "Say it Loud: I'm Black and I'm Proud." It was the summer fest 1968, and the Lake was crowded with people. That song seemed to indicate the new freedom black people had been looking for. Funny thing is, we had not found that freedom in speeches by Martin, or Revolution by Malcolm, or in the eloquence on the pages of novels written by James Baldwin. Nevertheless, it did come that hot, sticky, summer afternoon in the anthem shouted out by James Brown. Despite this, the President's assassination cast a pall over America. The Vietnam war was raging, the fight for civil rights and equality was being waged, and the president had been assassinated in office. The shit was broadcast live on television.

Change in the Air

I had sexual intercourse for the first time when I was 12. It was a terrifying experience, after the fact. It was also an unexpected act, completely out of the blue and opportunistic for the person who orchestrated the whole thing. If the exact same situation happened today, as it occurred at that time, and if it were found out, the perpetrator would be arrested and jailed. She was 18, I think. Further, my mom would go bananas had she known. My dad-I'm not sure how he would have reacted had he known, but my mom for sure would have been upset. The girl had been hired for the day as a babysitter for my brother Greg. It was through happenstance that I was home. The babysitter planned it all out and I was the lucky or rather, unlucky participant. I guess it depends on one's view.

My mom and dad had plans because my mom's relatives were coming to visit. My relatives came from the Midwest, Milwaukee, Wisconsin-and during their stay, one of the things to do was to go sightseeing. My parents, who were both working by that time, took a vacation for the duration of the family visit and took the relatives all around. Mostly the visitors were my aunts, my mom's sisters, and their kids, but sometimes my grandmother, or cousins of my mother visited. They'd did all the touristy stuff: Beverly Hills, Disneyland, the beaches and more.

On the day the event happened, my parents took my relatives to see movie star homes in Beverly Hills. Greg was ill. He was

4.5 at the time, and he wasn't able to go. My parents didn't want to cancel the trip, so they found a babysitter to sit with Greg for the day. Well, I'd been on that sightseeing trip before, so I opted out, and I asked if I could stay at home with Greg and the sitter. After some discussion and assurances that the sitter would be okay watching Greg I wasn't going to go buck wild, my parents felt it safe to go ahead with the plans.

Initially, everything was cool. But after my parents had been gone for about an hour, the sitter came into my bedroom, picked up Greg from his bed, and took him into my parents' bedroom, where she placed him in their bed. She came back to my room and said, "I want you to do something." She proceeded to take off her pants and expose to me the first vagina I had ever seen. This was in 1968 and all I could see was hair, everywhere. Then she told me to take off my pants. I froze, but I did as I was asked to do.

What I remember clearly from the episode was thinking I needed to obey what I was being told to do. The moment became exciting and frightening at the same time. She laid down on the bottom bunk bed and told me to climb on top of her. I did, and she put her hand on my penis and inserted me into her vagina. I had heard of doing that but, honestly, my friends and I, had not had even one conversation about that sort of thing prior to this event. My whole world, up to that time was little league baseball, street football, and whatever else. Sex, I mean real sex, wasn't even in my vocabulary. I had all sorts of thoughts going through my mind at the time. Mainly, I thought "This this thing of hers is wetter than a swimming pool." Another thought I had throughout it all was, "Am I going to be able to shower the sex smell off me before my parents get home?" The experience, while traumatizing after the fact was actually very exciting. I remember her body felt smooth and silky. My penis and I had no idea what we were doing, and she did all the work. I was just on top, moving my scrawny butt around and around in a circle, holding on for dear life. She had her eyes closed, but moved me up and down. I loved it, but afterwards, I took shower after shower trying to get the smell of sex off me.

As years passed, there were occasions when I saw the young lady here or there. I went out of my way to see her one time later, when I was about 22. She had grown into a very attractive woman, and I thought, "If she were to try that same ole same ole again now, I'd more than handle my own." She had children by then, and I know she would have won a rematch.

Here Comes Puberty

I grew into a popular young man during junior high school, and without knowing what I was doing, I found myself going steady with a girl. I guess it was a natural evolution of being popular that I had a girlfriend, and she was popular too. We did all the together things. I walked her to class, waited for her after school, and kissed her on the regular. I remember she was an excellent kisser, and I felt myself for sure too. I was among only a few of my friends who had girlfriends. She was fun to be with and she had a very funny sense of humor. She came from a big family and had older sisters, so she had the "know how to be social" thing going on in spades. She also, didn't have any hang-ups. I guess at 13, you really aren't old enough to have formed anything genuine. We were cool, and then at some point, we just moved on. I don't remember a break up at all; I just found myself without her one day, and so I, or we, kept it moving.

I had many friends on the block where I lived, both male and female. My main girl, Paula and I had been platonic friends forever, and she had a bunch of girlfriends. Sooner or later, there was a situation in which sex was discovered with one of those girlfriends. Sure enough, it wasn't long before one of her friends and I broke the thin ice between us and took to exploring each other in the natural. We were about 16 at the time. What I learned later, much later, was that this friend, was all-in on completing this exploration all along. She had plotted to get the deed done no matter what.

That fateful day was just like any other. I got home from school, and before doing anything else, went to the kitchen to do the dishes. My brother and I had a routine. If it was my week to wash, he had to dry and put the dishes away. If you had drying duties, you also had to sweep the kitchen. The next week we switched. So, I was in the kitchen with dish soap all over my hands when the door-bell rings. I went to the door, and hey, it was my girl, (an expression for someone I knew very well), so I said, "What's up? Come on in." She came in and I told her to take a seat in the kitchen while I finished the dishes. She told my brother that she'd dry them, freeing him up to go outside and play. We were in the kitchen talking and doing the dishes, and when I was done, she started pouring on the flirtation. She was cute and funny, and I was into it. But I asked, "Where is this coming from, because we're friends and we've been friends for years?" Flirting was common between us, and went back and forth with it all the time, but that time it was different. She had my attention, and before I knew it, we were kissing and making our way to my bedroom. I'd never done this before; I never gone into a bedroom with a girl while locking lips before. I was aroused for sure, and wasn't quite sure what to do when she suggested we have sex.

I said "Okay," so she got undressed and I got undressed. She laid down very still. Then I got on top of her, and we began to have sex. There was nothing sexy, romantic, or hot about it. We started moving together, and before I could quote my social security number, it was over. At least, for me it was.

She was still laying there, and she had figured it all out. She was a bit upset, as she told me I should have waited for her. "To do what?" I asked. We laid there naked and kissing for a while, and then she got up and left. Neither of us had any shame or regrets about any of it. I know this, because she told her best friend,

(Paula), who just happened to be my neighbor, and since Paula I were cool, she quizzed me about it all. We did the deed a few times after, and each time it was cool. This all took place around the time I was 16. She and I had been friends since grade school, and we remain friends today.

Paula, Priscilla, Phyllis, Pam, Doretha, and Sandra were a clique. They were Paula's besties, and by proxy, I was close to all of them, too. I often hung out with them whenever they went by Paula's which was often. My relationship with Paula dated back to kindergarten when at the very advanced age of five almost six I announced to Paula's mom and dad that I would walk her to school and keep her safe. I was officially her superman after that epic pronouncement. That was the beginning and foundation of our beautiful friendship, which is still as strong today as it was the day of that faithful pronouncement. Paula and I were way cool, and as we burned through our formative years, there were incidents that made for lifetime memories.

One Saturday afternoon, Paula, Phyllis and I, were in Paula's house smoking weed. Paula's mother and father were gone, and the expectation was they would be gone for hours. It was not unusual for us to do what we were doing whenever Paula's parents were out of the house and the opportunity presented itself. Mrs. O, Paula's mother, was my mom's best friend on the block. She was so cool and understanding. Anyone who knew Paula's mother instantly wished they had her for their mom. I cannot recall even one-time Mrs. O treated me any differently than like a beloved son. I ate breakfast, lunch, and dinner there whenever I wanted; I watched TV with the family, I hung out there all day, and Mr. and Mrs. O. damn near claimed me on their taxes. We were that close. And overall, our families were way cool. Her dad, Mr. O was a no-nonsense guy, much like my dad. He could roar like a mighty lion, but after all said and done, Mr. O loved his wife and kids and was as gentle as hand lotion. But that roar of his was spectacular, and it shook everything in the room to its foundation whenever it occurred.

Paula also had two brothers who I idolized, Darryl and Donald. Although they were older than me, Darryl and Donald always had time for me, no matter the subject, or anything going on for them. In effect, I had two older brothers I could count on for the things older brothers provide.

So, we were in the house, playing music and getting high, laughing, joking and whatever. I looked out the front window and saw Paula's parents pulling up outside. They were returning home hours earlier than expected. I knew it was not going to be good. I yelled, "Paula, here comes your mom and dad," and then I boned out-ran, scrammed, or took off-towards the back of the house. I ran through Paula's bedroom, through her brother's Darryl's bedroom, and out the back door. Paula had a dog, a big tan Afghan Hound with long hair and floppy ears, and lucky for me, he knew me. He was mostly docile, but he protected the family if needed. Well, when I burst through the back door, the dog, who had been lounging nearby, thought I was a burglar or something, because he immediately came for me. I had to stop and yell his name to get him to focus. I think he thought it was time to bite the crap out of someone, and that someone was me. But I calmed him down, by standing still and calling out his name. He stopped short of attacking me and let me pass. I was in the back-yard, when I heard the front door open and Paula's parents walk through the door. There was an almost immediate, "Goddammit what the hell is going on up in here?", from her father. That was my cue to climb the back fence, into the driveway and run across the street to my house. I sat outside on my lawn for about 30 minutes, and then went over to Paula's as if I were showing up for the first time. I knocked on the door and her father answered. I asked if Paula was there, and honestly, today I do not remember exactly what was said, but I do know I was not allowed to visit for a couple weeks. Mr. O did give me a look as if knew I had been a part of the shenanigans. But my girls, Paula and Phyllis, were so cool, they took the punishment all to themselves and did not rat me out. Talk about earning street cred. Paula and Phyllis were the definition of "ride or die."

Southern Roots

My dad's family was everywhere in our community. I had aunts, uncles, first cousins, second cousins, and close friends of the family who were "pretend cousins" because of family ties. It was as if I was related, in some way, to all of Pasadena. When I was growing up, it was nice to have family all over the city. Most of us cousins were close in age, and we were enrolled together throughout school. I never worried about getting into fights or having any harm done to me physically, because everyone knew me, and the consequences of someone doing harm to me or any family member of mine would have been riotous. It also, appeared as though everyone from my dad's community in Arkansas had gotten word that jobs and opportunity were plentiful out west, and thus migrated to California. I asked my dad how was it that he got to California, and he told me that his older brother, had gotten out of the Navy in San Diego, moved to Los Angeles and gotten a job immediately. In those days, anyone breathing who could walk on their own into a hiring office got hired. After my uncle had been in L.A. for a time, and had a wife and kids, he called my father and told him to get to California as soon as possible. I'm not certain how long it took for my dad to move west, but it must have been almost immediately, because shortly after he married my mom, they were in Pasadena, CA.

We moved to Altadena when I was five years old so, I don't really remember much about the early days in Pasadena. I do remember there were lots of kids around where we lived. Our street was Vernon Ave in an all-Black community. There had been a huge wave of migration from the South, and it just so happened that whole communities from Arkansas had gone west to California. No matter where we went, someone knew my dad or he knew somebody. This was in addition to his already huge family that, as I mentioned earlier, made the trek west. I also remember we lived near some train tracks and a school for children with physical disabilities and other special needs. I also recall there were a lot of homeless people near the train tracks where we lived. They were referred to as "bums" or "hobos" in those days. My brother and I played outside with other kids, and we were warned to stay away from the homeless. I don't believe they would have done any harm to us at that time. I believe the only thing they were trying to do was get a drink and stay comfortable. I feel pretty much the same way today. They're just down-on-their-luck people looking to survive as best they can.

The beautiful thing about growing up in a community filled with love is that you never realize the hardships endured by your parents, because the community supports everyone in it. I didn't realize that we didn't have much initially. I was always happy, fed, clothed, and loved. What more could I have asked for? I played outside with all the neighborhood kids from sun up to sun down every day, with not a care in the world.

I was out one evening at the Ritz Carlton Hotel in Pasadena, it's now been renamed to the Langham. I was there that particular evening because friends of mine were playing in the lounge, as a jazz band. I was at the bar, and someone I knew well walked in. He and I greeted each other warmly. We hadn't seen each other in years, but our recognition was immediate because of the number of years we had been friends. We started talking, and I reminded him that we went as far back as kindergarten, and to my surprise, he said "What do you mean, Kenny? We go back to Vernon Avenue in Pasadena." My mouth fell wide open. He recalled that we had been neighbors before kindergarten, which meant we were as young as three, four or five years old. I was stunned, but in the best way possible.

I do recall, with some certainty our move to Altadena. The move was huge; for Myron and me it meant no longer sleeping in a crammed bedroom with just one other room in the house to roam. The new place was a palace compared to where we had been living. I don't know what went through the heads of my parents, but it was a meaningful step. The day we were shown the house as a family, my dad, mom, brother, and I rode up to the house with a real estate agent. When we turned onto the street, I thought we were in paradise. It was the same as the homes we looked at when we went sightseeing. It still had not registered that my parents were about to look at a house they'd eventually buy. We pulled up to the house, and the real estate guy parked the car and turned off the engine. We got out of the car and walked up to what I believed, at that age was a mansion. My mom and dad went into the house with the real estate guy, and my brother and I played on the expansive front lawn. We ran up and down a gentle slope and marveled at the fully-grown Magnolia tree in the front. At some point we were called around to the backyard by our parents. At 5.5 years old, it looked like a full baseball field to me. I remember being happy at the thought of moving into that house.

As I said before, Myron and I were happy kids, up to that point in time, and we were well adjusted and enjoyed our lives and time on Vernon Ave. in Pasadena. But the awe of taking on a house of our own overwhelming. The house felt, at the time, big enough to get lost in.

Then, at some not long after we moved into the house my mom had Greg. I don't even recall her being pregnant, I just know that one day, I came home from school and there was a new kid in the house. I guess my parents really celebrated the purchase of the new house, and Greg was the result of the celebration. At that point there were five of us: mom, dad and us three hard-headed boys.

Together, we did family things, and one of them was to taking car cruises through Beverly Hills. We piled into the car and made our way to what we called the "rich people section of town." At that time, there were real television and movie stars. We saw the homes of Lucille Ball, Merv Griffin, Dean Martin, Johnny Carson, Sammy Davis Junior, and more; the list could go on and on as to who was who in Hollywood at that time, and we believed all of them lived in Beverly Hills. We routinely drove over there, bought a map of the stars' homes and went neighborhood to neighborhood burning up gas looking at houses. It ranked as my all-time number one favorite trip. On the way home we drove past Orange Grove Boulevard, in Pasadena, through an area known as Millionaire's Row. Myron and I pointed out which house was going to be ours when we grew up. My imagination was endless at that time.

I don't remember a time we went without. We were not rich, by a long shot, but we were not poor, either. As I said before my parents stretched for us. They took everything they had and made it work for the benefit of our family. Today, I liken it to the parable of Jesus feeding the multitudes with two fish and five loaves of bread. I've heard it said, "The truth can be stranger than fiction," and in that sense, I witnessed the miracle of my parents every day.

Baseball was the sport of choice for my Dad, and he saw to it that each of his sons was duly baptized in the sport. We took amazing trips to Dodger stadium every season. Without fail, we saw at least three games every year. My dad, his friends, and his brother in law, Uncle George, took all of us boys to the games. Usually, they were Saturday games, and if we were lucky, we saw a double header. A day game was followed 90 minutes later by a twilight game. Man, those games were the highlight of our summers. It was usually my dad; his best friend "Doe Shaker," or Mr. Allison; Uncle George; me, Myron, and Greg; and our cousins, Maurice, Tim, Andrew, and Herman. We were in Dodger stadium. In addition, we all played the game and knew it well, so we were right at home sitting and talking ball. Plus, I could never forget the best part of the trip: getting "Dodger dogs, peanuts, and sodas." Those were the good 'ole days. I imagine those trips cost my dad nearly a week's wages. It's another way he and my mom made sacrifices for my siblings and me.

Another family outing was visiting relatives on Dad's side of the family. His sisters, one older and one younger, lived on the same street, about four houses from each other. Between them, I had eight cousins, but I also knew all the kids in the neighborhood, where they lived, and what kids were in the surrounding area, so when we went to visit family, we were golden. We couldn't wait to get out of the car to begin playing with our cousins and running up and down the street, wilding out. Every few minutes, my aunts, my mother, or somebody else yelled at us to get the hell out of the street or calm the hell down. It was a wild and crazy time.

I especially looked forward to hanging out with my cousin Maurice. He and I were 10 months apart in age, but Morris, as we called him, was a big brother as much as he was a cousin. He was cool and he ran around with older dudes in his neighborhood, which gave him an older air. He was also a stud athlete in two sports, baseball and basketball, and knew everyone who was anyone in the city. I knew his friends in his neighborhood, and those I didn't know, he introduced to me. We always had a gang of fun when I visited.

One thing that happened a lot, but not enough for either of us, was sleepovers. During visits to my aunt's house, Morris and I made sure to ask our parents if he could stay overnight at our house. We almost always asked if it was the weekend. He came up to our house and hung out with me and my crew in our neighborhood.

Everyone on my street knew Morris. It was a good switch up for both of us from time to time.

He and I were one grade apart in school. By grade 11, Morris gave up baseball to play basketball full time. It was a good move for him, as he went on to become an all-American in high school in the guard position, and he received offers with full ride – athletic scholarships to most colleges in America. He chose a school relatively close to home in a conference where the family could see him play during the televised games.

I always observed Morris because he was an important figure in my life growing up. With my curiosity and observations, I picked up some valuable life information early on. I call the information, jewels because it's about lifestyle choices. We must have been ahead of our times in some areas because that information is still with me today. One of the longest lasting gifts I received from Morris was an introduction to the fine arts. Through Morris, I developed an interests in Jazz, Fashion and Art.

These interests have had a profound influence on my life. He introduced me to jazz when I was about 12 years old. Most of the people in my inner circle at that time were listening to the Motown sound, the Philly sound, Memphis sound, and other R&B in the mid-to late 60s and into the 70s. There were countless music acts, singers and other performers at that time. We went to legendary house parties and danced to the sounds of the Temptations, Stevie Wonder, Marvin Gaye, Diana Ross and the Supremes, Curtis Mayfield, and Al Green, and we danced fast and slow watching and getting the latest dance moves from shows such as *Soul Train*. But I remember visiting my cousin, as I did probably once every other week, when he pulled a stack of records and began playing them for me on a tiny record player. I listened. He began speaking to me about new music he and his friends were listening to: Miles Davis, John Coltrane, Thelonious Monk, Bud Powell, and more. He said, "Cousin, you need to pick you up some jazz." He spoke in that vernacular. That's all he said. I had a light album collection at home at the time. I think I was also listening to the Delfonics, the Jackson 5, and the Ohio Players. So, I went home, grabbed my savings from my allowance, and figured out a way to buy my first Miles Davis album, "*Kind of Blue.*" I must have played the vinyl off that record. I sat in my room playing the album over and over and over until I could hum the entire work and each note in it. I was hooked, not only by the music, but also by the genre, because it had been recommended to me by my cousin, who I revered. Jazz is an important element in my life today.

Morris also introduced me to fashion. He had the classic male model frame; he was 6'3" tall and slim, and he fit easily into a nice suit. I always admired his style and fashion sense. I was talking with his mother, my aunt Myrlean, one day, and I asked, "Auntie, where does Morris get his fashion sense?" She just smiled and looked at me over her glasses. In her own way, she was telling me that she was the genius behind the styling. She could be wicked funny when she wanted to be. No argument from me. Morris also taught me not to be a billboard for designers, i.e., you'll never catch me walking around with a big designer's name plastered across my chest on a t shirt, or any piece of clothing for that matter. He said, "They aren't paying you, so why give them free advertisement?" I loved it. I do admit to the occasional t shirt with athletic logo.

Today, Morris has a college degree in fine arts, specifically interior design. He's decorated his various homes and spaces with really nice art and photos. I've managed to pick up a few pieces over the years, and it's always nice when I get a nod of approval on my selections.

My dad was crazy about his family, wife, kids, sisters, brothers, aunts, uncles, and cousins… Family was a theme for my dad. He and his siblings were as thick as thieves and seemed to always enjoy each other's company. My father used to say to me, "Boy, there is no substitute for family." It took me a minute, but I've come to accept that mantra now that I have my own family.

Dad had loads of friends, too. I'm telling you, every Negro he knew in Arkansas must have come west. There were Willie Bluford, or Blu; Quentin Stepps, or Lil Stepps; Doe-Shaker, or Doree Allison; and Hamp, Pudge, Calvin McGruder, and a host of other names. When they all got together, which they did, on occasion, it was a riot. They had stories to tell, most of them lies, and the laughing and shouting went on and on. My dad loved him some Arkansas Black folk and they loved him back.

Casserole

Terrace Street, the street on which I grew up, was a mixture of everything. I can see, looking back on my youth, all the loved poured out onto us kids, those who lived on the street and those who visited us on the street. While we lived on a cul de sac with three different street names, what was the coolest was that everyone knew everyone, literally. One year one of the neighbors who was more artistically inclined decided to ask all the neighbors to take part in a Christmas nativity themed light show for our block. Almost every neighbor said yes, and the display brought a lot of attention to our tiny little street for years to come during the holidays.

Mr. J, lived next door to us, and he was a Los Angeles County Deputy Sheriff. But he was also one of the resident artists for the County Sheriff Department. He came up with the idea to make individual Christmas trees out of plywood that could be posted on every yard in our cul de sac. Further, he spelled out "Merry Christmas," and "Happy New Year," along with other themes from around the Christmas holidays and each house got a letter of the alphabet to go with its tree. The idea was that people would come from all over to see this Christmas display in our neighborhood. The Christmas trees had cutouts in the front for lights. It was a novel idea and just about every house participated. There were hold outs who did not participate, but most did. When Mr. J completed the work, the neighborhood put it up and the people came. I think the display went up around December 15th,” and we kept it up until a few days after the new year. The display went up for years. We were quite avant-garde.

The neighborhood was full of characters. We had one kid who could not keep himself out of juvenile hall even though he came from one of the more well-to-do families. His father was a respected city worker and his mother was an entrepreneur before the word was fashionable. I don't think his mother ever held a nine to five job. She had a keen understanding of a certain type of business, and as such, she opened business after business. She was an original mover and shaker in the community. I recall her letting me work and earn money with her from time to time if I was free on weekends. Her son, who worked with her on occasion, in one her stores, asked me to hang out and work the store with him. It was so cool. I was behind the cash register ringing up pops, candy, and the sort on a Saturday afternoon, and having a ball as if I were Mr. Important. Her son could have cared less. He hated it, even though he had nothing better to do. He was a smart but mischievous young man.

Then there was the white kid (deliberately specific) who hailed from a family of five; mom, dad and three kids. He was the only boy and the baby of the family. Talk about spoiled-that kid could do no wrong, but in his defense, he hadn't a prejudiced bone in his body, and he played basketball as if he were born with a ball in his hand. He stood about 6'5" and could beat any combination of two or three of us together on any given day of the week. We used to play in his backyard, and I cannot remember winning a game. He was killed in an automobile accident in his early 20s. It was a tragic accident that took the life of someone who lived larger than life and who was loved by family and friends.

Another of my childhood friends from the neighborhood passed away much too early: Peter. He was a long-haul driver who lived in Texas. He was murdered. Peter was born on October 31st, and as we grew up, he was subjected to all sorts of cruel jokes solely because he was born on Halloween. Peter was an excellent mechanic and a great friend. He had a natural inclination for anything mechanical. He and I were nearly two years apart, Peter being older than me. He had a sister named L. L. was fine, but we hardly saw her while we were growing up. She tended to stay in the house close to her mother and didn't really like to come out and play with the rest of the neighbors. L was older than Peter by two years.

They were bi-racial. Their mom was white and their father was black. Their mother, Pat, was quiet and very friendly. I went over to their house all the time to play with Peter or to get him to come outside. Peter's father was easy going but could turn on a dime and be a real hot-head. He was nice enough on the surface, but that Black man had some issues. One time, a neighbor was backing out of his driveway and came really close to hitting Mr. P's car. He stopped just short of hitting the car. He got out of the car to see how much room he still had, determined he'd better pull up, and started again. After another try, he backed out successfully and pulled off down the street. As soon as he was out of ear distance, Mr. P went into this tirade suggesting that he'd kill that motherfucker if he had hit his car! I thought "Goddamn, man; it really wasn't that serious. This is someone you've known for 20 years and now you're ready to kill him if he accidentally pings your ride. WTF."

L got pregnant around age 18 and I thought Mr. P was going to murder the brotha responsible. He was livid like a MF, and would have killed the brotha if he had enticed him to go to his house. I think homeboy read the writing on the wall and decided against a face to face with Mr. P.

Mr. P had another, older son name Paul, who lived in Alabama with his mother, but would come out to visit from time to time. He was older than L and Peter, but not too much older. For some reason, all of us in the neighborhood got along well although our age differences were as much as eight years apart. But there were so many kids on the block, you always had someone your age to play with.

The last family to move into the neighborhood and be considered a part of my block was the Williams family. There were Mr. and Mrs. Williams, their daughter G, and their sons Richard and Michael. They fit right in and became a part of the everyday chaos as if they had been there since day one. I remember the day they moved in. I was 11, and their son Michael had just turned 12 and was a few months older than me. I was friends with both sons, but Richard and I shared years of mischievous deeds during our teenage and young adult years.

The first school I attended was Edison elementary. It was less than one mile from my house. I, along with every other kid in the neighborhood, walked to and from school each day. Back in those days, in the early 60s it was commonplace for kids to walk everywhere. The dangers of strangers and others of their ilk were either not easily identifiable or nonexistent. The idea that someone would abuse you, kidnap you, or mess with you in any unnatural way was not a consideration at all. Although I'm sure they were out there lurking.

I'm walking home from school one day, Robin B; we lived on the same cul de sac, and he was four days older than me, but one grade above me. I had the same situation with another neighbor, Vincent. Vincent was eight days older but he, too, was one grade above me. We were all born in the month of December. School started each year in September, and there was a rule that prohibits students from entering school if they were four years old, due to turning five after Nov. 30th. The birthday cutoff rule kept me out of school as my birthday fell into the second week of Dec. Robin's birthday fell into the second week of Dec., too; however, Vince's birthday was within the first week. At any rate, they were one grade ahead of me.

So, I was on my way home from school with Robin. We were probably around nine at the time, and as we reached my street, we could see a police car parked at the corner. Actually, it was a sheriff's vehicle. We did not have police officers because we were not a city; we lived in an unincorporated portion of LA county, so we had sheriffs. As we walked past the vehicle, the cop said, "Come here," to me and Robin. We asked, "For what?" and he said, "Where are you going?" and we responded, "We're going home." Once again, he said, "Come here," but we kept walking, and as we got past him, we began to run and we did run, all the way to Robin's house. We ran there because Robin's father was a cop-an LAPD cop. If some shit was going to jump off, then let it jump off near or at Robin's doorstep. Looking back, I believe Robin and I did the right thing by running away. Something in my bones tells me that officer was probably some kind of pervert who was looking to molest us or harm us in some way. I know he had bad intentions, and I felt it in my bones at the time.

I picked up some bad habits right as I hit my teens. The first bad habit was smoking cigarettes. I used to sneak cigarettes from my dad when I was about 13. It started as most bad habits do: I did it just for fun. Low and behold, it began a journey of me becoming a cigarette smoker. I wasn't encouraged to smoke, nor can I really recall a reason other than teenage mischief, but it turned into a habit. My mom and dad both smoked when Myron and I were young, but my mom quit long before Greg was born. My dad continued his smoking habit. I'd sneak a cigarette from my dad's pack and go someplace alone or with Peter, my neighbor, and we'd smoke the cigarette. Peter would steal cigs from his dad as well. I never got sick smoking, and maybe if I had gotten sick, that nasty habit never would have gotten a hold of me. But I didn't get sick, and it did get a hold of me.

I had a hell of a battle in my attempts to quit smoking, and finally, after many failed attempts, I was able to quit. Smoking cigarettes, in my opinion, is the most addicting habit one can have. And this opinion is coming from someone who's had a lot of addictions. Cigarette smoking in and of itself is bad enough, but then it is often associated with various other socially accepted recreational activities, such as drinking. The road to quitting smoking is difficult and the use of all self-discipline is needed if there is any real effort. Therefore, being able to quit also means shifting associations away from smoking. It is much easier said than done. In addition to the physical and mental associations, of smoking there is the actual addiction to the nicotine. So, while the body is craving for the next "hit," the mind is associating some relevant activity to go along with it. It really is a bitch of a time trying to quit.

I had a very difficult time wrapping my head around how powerfully addicting cigarettes could be. Retailers that sell tobacco must make a killing (no pun intended) pushing the disease of addiction, and the related illnesses. I guess anything in the name of money. Shortly after learning how to smoke and inhale, I started smoking marijuana. Now that was definitely worth the price of admission. There were no associated headaches, lung coughs, or any of that, when smoking marijuana. I just got high, laughed my ass off, and bought cheeseburgers from the local vendor, Mr. Eskridge at his corner store.

There was another mischievous deed I'd discovered as a teen. One time, my dad was injured at work. The injury was serious, and he was hospitalized for nearly two weeks. At his job, toxic chemicals were used. Apparently, some of the chemicals got onto his skin, specifically his legs, and the chemicals began to eat away at his flesh. My mom went to the hospital nightly to visit him. I was 15 or 16 at the time. There were us brothers then and we had two cars. One evening, as my mom was preparing to visit my dad, she asked me to start one of the cars and back it out so that she could use the other one. The car she asked me to move was a 1955

Chevy. You could put the key in the ignition, turn it over a bit to the right, then turn the car all the way over without needing a key the rest of the way. In addition, the car could run without the key in the ignition. This was a wonderful discovery for me, because I was chomping at the bit to drive. I knew I could, or that I had the knowledge how, but I had not gotten a chance. I knew that as soon as my mom left for the hospital that evening, I would hop in the car, turn the ignition to where a key was no longer needed, and take the car and go joy riding.

I did that very thing. I got the car backed down the driveway onto the street, and I was gone. I repeated this several times when my mom was gone. I would not stay gone long, and I did not do any risky driving. It was risky enough just doing what I did. I was under age, had no license, and was driving around with friends. This was just an example of how different I was from the model taught to me by my parents.

About the time I discovered these vices-car thieving, cigarettes and marijuana-I was barely out of junior high school. You may be getting the picture that my parents paid little to no attention to what was going on, but nothing could be further from the truth. I was as sneaky as any growing teenager and my parents were very conservative and strict. I did not have paid admission to do anything I wanted or to go anywhere I wanted. I needed permission to go and do things, and if I did not get permission beforehand, there was a cost associated with that. My household was no different from most Black or African American households. We got punished for misbehavior and punishment, and that sometimes meant having a belt taken to your ass. Ass whoopings like the ones I got as a child will cost a parent at least one night in jail and a hearing in front of a judge nowadays.

Black n White

We were a family that attended church every Sunday; going to church was a staple. The Black church served the whole of the community in the days I was growing up. There was the community in which you lived, and there was your church community. The thing to know about the Black church is that anyone and any community can be served. Its purpose is to heal, unify, and teach, and that purpose can't be met if it's reserved for Blacks only. The Black church has never been just about the black experience. All are welcome though I refer to it here as the Black church because in the days I was growing up, there were not a lot of integrated churches. But from the teachings I heard on Sundays, the thing most desired was the saving of souls-all souls, and not just Black ones.

As a family, we all got dressed on Sunday mornings and we headed off to church. My parents made sure we arrived in time for Sunday school, and then we stayed for Sunday service. I attended one of the first black churches in my city, and it was one of the most popular churches, in the city too. In 1966 or early 1967, Dr. Martin Luther King visited our church. I can't remember much about the event today, but I do know it was a much talked about affair before he came and after he left. So, the notion that I did what I wanted willy-nilly is false. I was a mischievous kid doing mischievous things at a time in my life when that behavior was normal.

I do have and live with regrets. I know saying as much is awful. And it is an awful admission because it's true. To know that you haven't lived your best life is difficult to digest. I knew well the difficulties Blacks faced in the late 60s and 70s when I was coming of age, and yet, I still did not apply myself and all that I had to offer. What is clear to me is that some early behaviors altered my path and stunted my development. I'm cool with who I am today, but I'm not resting.

I was in a very confused mental state around the time I was entering high school. I had no self-identity, nor did I have a clue about anything in the world other than my friends, wanting to just be popular, go to parties, and smoke weed. I wasn't typical, but I wasn't alien either.

I went out for the football team as a freshman. I made the "C" team, which was comprised of freshmen and sophomores. And I not only made the team but was also a quasi-star. I played quarterback and defensive back and I was good at both positions. I wasn't afraid of contact sports, and since I'd been involved in sports all my life, participation was normal to me. Our coach was Mr. Palmer. He thought I showed a lot of promise as an athlete, and because he did, he used me a lot and kept me on the field.

I had a great freshman experience playing football that year. I went out for the team again as a 10th grader, and again I made the team. I was a second-string quarterback and a first-string defensive back. I was a real ball hawk as a defensive back and while my hitting and tackling was suspect, I had a knack for reading the opposing quarterback and being in position to make interceptions. I again made the team my junior year and was a real star on the junior varsity. One memorable game for me was played at Pasadena City college and my dad attended. I had two interceptions that night, and one almost ran back for a touchdown. I was very proud of my effort that evening, and my dad was beaming after the game. He was in a good mood, and I imagine he was very proud of me as well. I should have been a lock for varsity and a starting position but I did not make the team. It was a crushing blow to me and my ego at the time, but I pretended that I was not bothered by the snub.

I recall my parents asking me if I wanted them to intervene on my behalf. I said no. If I look at that situation objectively today, I can find reasons why I was left off the team, and honestly my talent, ability, and commitment were just as big as others who were there, so it must have been something completely out of my control as to why I did not make the team. It was also humiliating and embarrassing and one of the single greatest letdowns in all my life. Thank you very much, Coach Hamilton, for your personal contribution to what was at the time the single biggest letdown in my life.

I had a girlfriend in my sophomore and junior years of high school. She was from a very prominent family in the community, and she was a star in her own right. She was a very talented athlete. I don't recall how our getting together happened; I only know that it did, and when it did – bam! What a togetherness. I can say without a doubt I was in love. I was old enough to drive when we met, and I could drive my parents' car on occasion, but not every day. So, seeing her during the week and on weekends meant either walking to her house or taking public transportation. We lived about five miles away from each other. The good thing was that it was mostly a straight line for the whole five miles. The relationship was innocent enough initially. I mean, we were two 16-year-olds fumbling around trying to figure out our biology at a time when the opposite sex is coming into plain view. And it had to be innocent enough for our parents to allow it to progress. Both she and I had parents who wielded a very strong influence over our lives at the time. Additionally, she came from a big family of older brothers and an older sister and they were definitely all up in our soup. But it was all cool. I opted, most of the time, to walk to her house. We'd make plans for a Saturday, and if neither of us had individual sports or family activities, I'd take the 5 mile walk to her house and spend all day there. Talk about love. Sometimes we'd go to the movies ahead of the chaos of a Sunday night and actually see the movie. Every now and again, we'd get out on a Sunday night to Cinema 21 and be with the crowd.

My parents liked my girl and thought the idea of me having a girlfriend was acceptable, funny, and cool. My parents were not that much older than me; therefore, they were young enough to process the circumstances in a way that made sense to them. My girlfriend's parents were cool, too. I liked them a lot. We broke up at the beginning of my senior year of high school. It was all my doing, and one of the dumbest mistakes of my young life at the time. She told me I'd regret it, and I did. She stuck by me, even though I made a lackluster effort in my academics, did not play varsity football, and smoked a lot of weed, not to mention the other assorted juvenile behaviors that stuck to me like a bee to honey. Talk about Wonder Woman; she fit the bill completely. Shortly after our break up, she started dating a guy a year older, and they went on to get married and the whole nine yards.

From the beginning, I was a popular one. I can't say I know or knew why, but I always had friends, lots of them. They were both boys and girls, and the common thing was they were all popular in their own way. My friends had friends, lots of them.

By the time I reached high school, my inner circle was cemented. They were guys with whom I'd do everything and go everywhere. If you saw me, I was with one if not all of the following: Stanley, Freddie, Richard, Tony, Jerome, and Bobby. They were my original "ride or die" clique. We were a collective, but I had amazing one-on-one friendships one on one with each of them.

The Clique

S tan and I cannot see each other without laughing before any words are spilled. Ours is a very rich and treasured history full of love between two people as life-long friends. We spent thousands of hours together during our formative years, and there isn't just one incident that defined our friendship; it's a collective of 50 plus years now that we've known each other. One thing that can be said about Stan is that he is loyal to a fault. If you ever had a friend in Stan, you'll always have one. If he says he's got your back, believe it. Loyalty is his hallmark. His personal journey, aside from his willingness to be steadfast in his friendship with me has enriched my life beyond measure. He is a treasured friend to my entire family.

Fred is, for me, one of the funniest human beings alive. He and I have been friends since the beginning of high school, and have remained so throughout the years. As we've gotten older, I am able to fully appreciate the wisdom of Fred, in the everyday conversations we share. He has always shown me brotherhood and friendship. Fred, our friend Tony Thomas, and I worked at a huge retail store after high school graduation. We were hired as seasonal workers with a chance to stay on if we wanted to at the end of the holiday season. I remember with disdain having to help setup for Halloween by setting out a bunch of pumpkins. As we moved further into the holiday season towards Thanksgiving and Christmas, the store was a madhouse with shoppers everywhere every day. We three worked in various departments throughout the store, but could be found mostly at the cashier registers bagging merchandise after purchases had been made. We worked an afternoon to closing shift, essentially 1:00 p.m. to 10:00 p.m. Fred and I had cars, and one of us always made sure Tony had a ride to work. Many days we just all rode to work together. The pay was minimum wage, but it was enough for gas, lunch money, and weed, the three essentials. During our lunch break, we'd head outside, usually to the back of the store, spark up a couple of joints, and then return to the store, high as a kite, and manage through to 10:00 p.m. One evening, during a very busy weekend, we took our normal lunch break at 6:00 p.m. Tony and Fred had been complaining about the working conditions and about how much they were being sweated by the supervisor. We were walking and talking our way to the northern end of the store parking lot. Construction for a freeway was underway and we could go up near the construction site and never be seen once it got dark. We had just started smoking when Fred started going off on how much he hated the place and the manager. We agreed the manager was an asshole. The more we discussed the situation, the more Fred got upset. It probably didn't help that we were two joints in by this time. Tony and I were cracking up and trying to get our smoke on. Fred said, "Fuck it you guys let's quit." Tony and I thought about it and we said. "Okay" because the plan wasn't to stay there forever. We figured we'd finish out the month and then quit after Christmas. This was just after Thanksgiving. Fred said, "No, I mean let's quit right fucking now. Let's not go back after lunch." In other words, he was suggesting we ghost our jobs right then and there. We started laughing even harder, which I know was the weed, but said. "Yeah okay" to quitting right then and there. We finished the weed and split. Never went back.

I met Richard through Stan. Stan had always talked about his cousin Richard, but I had never met him. Richard lived in

Pasadena, and we lived in Altadena. Not too far from each other, but far enough that when you're young, unless you have a car, it's too far to walk. One Saturday afternoon, I was at Stan's house when Richard and Jeffrey showed up. Jeff is Richard's younger brother. Needless to say, we hit it off instantly.

Richard, Stanley, and I were out one night, partying and looking for parties. I am about six months older than Richard and Stanley; they were 17 at the time of this incident, and I was 18. We had gone to a couple of parties in Pasadena, earlier in the evening, and both parties had been duds. Someone, told us there was a house party on Loma Alta Drive in Altadena. There was something different, better even, about house parties in Altadena. For some reason, the geographical area had something to do with whether or not the party was going to be worth attending. And in those days, it was easy to crash a party. An invitation was not anything you worried about. We knew a house party on Loma Alta in Altadena was going to have some fine honeys up in there, and that was just the start. There were also going to be lots of folks holding weed. But Stan, Richard, and I never had a lack for weed, so we were going to show up simply for the honeys. There was the great chance you are going to get nice cross section of honeys from all over the city and its high schools. For sure Muir and PHS were going to have representation at the party. And then there would be folks from PCC and Blair H.S. in the house too.

So, we headed up to where there was supposed to be a party. It was almost 11:00 p.m. Richard was driving his mother's car. Out of nowhere, a sheriff's car pulled in behind us and started following us. Richard's car was full of that loud (marijuana), so we began to put it out as fast as possible. Then, like clockwork, the sheriff put the lights on us. "Uh oh," we thought, "there's smoke all over the car." Richard pulled over to a stop. The cops come up, smelled the weed, and immediately began to pull us from the car. The main sheriff, the one barking all the fucking orders was a short, stout, Italian by the name of Capezio. He was going off like a motherfucker. He and his partner put us up against their car and told us not to move. They then proceeded to tear the car apart looking for the weed. Luckily for us, most of it had already been smoked. I say most because I jammed a joint in my mouth as soon as the lights hit us. So, they looked and looked and found nothing. Capezio, came back to the car where we were standing. He just stared at us, then held his flashlight up to our faces and told us "Open your mouths." Stan and Richard opened their mouths so wide I could see their tonsils. I was reluctant because I had weed everywhere in my mouth. Capezio came closer and ordered, "I said, open your mouth." I did, and I'm sure it looked as if I had broccoli wrapped in toilet tissue in my mouth. Capezio started yelling at me, "Spit it out! Spit it out!" and I started spitting out the weed on the sheriff's car. He said, "Get that shit off my car." Now during this whole time, a junior officer on the scene mostly observed. He did most of the car search, but at that point, he was just watching. Not only was he African American, but I knew him! I say that vaguely because I did know him, but he did not know me. He had just married my next-door neighbor's oldest daughter, and I had attended the wedding with my mother.

I recognized him as soon as I got out of the car, when I was made to stand next to their vehicle. He was very distinctive looking, because his face was heavily freckled. Even though I instantly knew who he was, I said nothing. When it looked as though Capezio was about to rock and roll with me though and possibly hit me or something, I let out that I knew that officer, and I began to give details about his wedding, reception, family, in-laws, and more. I had lived next door to the woman who was now his wife for at least 12 years before they were married. I knew her and her entire family very well. She was the oldest of three children, two of them girls and one boy. Her brother and I were fast friends, and her Dad was the guy who made the Christmas ornaments for our block. In addition to that, her father was also an LA county sheriff and liked me a lot. When I was done reading the younger officer's whole life story, he intervened in the situation which looked as if it were about to get ugly. Officer Capezio let us go, but told us that since Richard and Stan were 17, we had to get off the streets immediately. It was after 10:00 p.m. and he was trying to enforce the "10:00 p.m." curfew on us. We said "Okay," but stayed out anyway.

Tony was a professor. He got higher than anybody. Tony would smoke with you, drink with you, and then teach you calculus in the abstract. We had to say, "Shut the fuck up, Tony; ain't nobody trying to be Einstein right about now." But he couldn't help it; He was just smart. He was fun, too.

Tony and I went to the military together. We got tired of our days playing out the same every day, with the only highlight copping some weed and smoking. After an analysis of the options available to us, we decided to enlist, taking advantage of the buddy-buddy system. Basic training and advanced individual training, (AIT) were great since we were together and then we went our separate ways to serve. We stayed in touch, and eventually both left the service under honorable conditions and returned home. Tony passed away in 2012, which hurt my heart something fierce. Richard called me while I was in Saudi Arabia and told me that Tony had been taken to a hospital and that it was serious. We spoke about it, and he promised to call me back with an update. I received a call hours later from Greg and my mom. They told me Tony had passed away. RIP, Tony. I love you.

I met Tom Sahm in high school. We might have been freshmen or sophomores-but not any older than 15. Tom and I were cool right from jump-street, that is from the beginning. We were both affable and easy going, and we both like to get high. I smoked with Tom all the time at school, after school, and any other time. He may not know this, but I really enjoyed my relationship with Tom, it was different from the ones I had in the neighborhood. We got high and talk about crazy shit, or do crazy shit, like jump in the damn next to the Sierra Madre Golf Course and swim around. Or he'd drive over to my house from East Pasadena, or Sierra Madre, pick me up, and take me over to his place to party with friends and drink and smoke. I remember that just before I left for the Army, Tom and I went to Eaton Canyon in Altadena, and walked, smoked, and just talked about life. It was one of the last conversations I had with him. I don't know that I've seen him since.

Not to be left out is Jerome, also known as WJS, Bobby Wilson, - Lil Will, Jack Bridges, and a couple more nicknames. Something I had in common with him and all of my friends was that each person's mother was my mother and my mother, was their mother. During the time of my youth, a community village- neighbors, teachers, aunts, and uncles looked after everyone, especially the kids.

Time Flies-Literally

I spent four years in high school as an official slacker. It's an admission I deeply regret today. I went to classes as needed, but I did not study, nor did I apply myself. I was under the influence of a distorted sense of reality that continued to tell me that everything was okay, even when it wasn't. I knew that what I was doing was wrong, ditching class day after day after day, but I hadn't the inner fortitude to stop. The shame of it all was that had I applied myself, I might have salvaged a GPA good enough to have my choice of school after high school graduation. I can't blame my recklessness on anyone other than myself. In many regards, I was the ring leader.

A few days before high school graduation, I was in a car with a few of my friends, and we were doing what we normally did, which was smoking weed. It was early June; school was just about out, and everyone had summer fever. We couldn't wait to leave high school, and those last few days were just "show up and hang out" days. My high school was adjacent to a well-known park. I could find students in the park every school day of every school year ditching one class or another. On that particular day my friends and I were parked in the parking lot of this park, adjacent to the school. Someone in the car noticed a Frito-Lay snack truck in the parking lot in very close proximity to where we were. It so happened that the driver of the truck had left the back door of the vehicle open. We got out of the car, and proceeded to fill our vehicle with every kind of potato chip, Dorito chip, cracker, and cookie we found inside the truck. We had boxes of chips that we piled into the trunk of our car. Soon after we loaded up the trunk of our car, the driver returned, hopped directly into his truck and drove off. He hadn't an inkling that his truck had been robbed. We sat there in the car, smoking weed and munching on the snacks.

We were completely unaware that we were being surrounded by police cars. Without any notice whatsoever, the police began knocking on our windows and telling us to get out. We were truant and we were smoking a load of weed. Also, unbeknownst to any of us at the time, we had smoked all the weed. The police persisted with the window knocking, and we sat and chatted amongst ourselves as we tried to think it through. There was no way we were going to get away. The car was blocked in and there were police officer's standing all around the car. I didn't know about everyone else, but my high was blown; I was completely sober and scared. We determined there wasn't any more weed in the car-not a joint, not a roach, nothing- just ashes and four brothas who were high. We opened the doors and the smoke poured out. The officers were pissed because we had made them wait. They immediately pulled out handcuffs and cuffed us one to another. They started tearing the car apart looking for evidence. I looked at my friends, and needless to say, we were all bone sober. The only thing I could think about was that I was scheduled to graduate high school in a few days. But barring a miracle, that was all going out the window because I was about to be arrested. On top of it all, I was 18 so I was going to county jail. "Holy hell," I thought, "I'm not built for jail." So, the cops called other cops because they couldn't believe there was no weed to be found. As we had become aware that we had smoked everything, it became quite funny. We didn't have any more weed, which meant that since that couldn't box up the putrefied air as evidence, they'd have to let us go, and that's exactly what happened. They were as mad as mad could be. We walked. Before we were able to leave, the officers who were on scene opened the trunk of the car and found the boxes of chips and cookies. They began calling around to the local stores to see if any of them had been vandalized. They got nothing-nada, zilch, and zero.

There was no justifiable excuse for my behavior. I continued to push boundaries and had already survived at least three encounters of the same kind in which the outcome could have been me going to jail. Who was I pretending to be? I was not capable of doing three minutes in jail, let alone real time.

The shame of my behavior was that my parents were good parents, loving parents, who sacrificed time, money, and any and everything they had on my behalf, and I was out in the streets acting like a wild animal. My parents trusted me and loved me more than anything. I was beyond being punished because of my age and perceived adulthood. Nevertheless, I had not processed how much hurt my parents would endure if something were to happen to me, such as jail or worst. They knew nothing of my indiscretions. Put another way, they knew nothing of the degree of my indiscretions. My parents weren't ones to bury their heads in the sand. No, my parents were more likely to bury their feet in my ass. But they were the opposite of over-bearing. As I got older, they became more fun for me, because I could understand them, and in turn they showed me that they had always understood me. They took the reins off and let me do my own thing, but I was not acting with the responsibility I was given. I was abusing the trust given to me.

My parents sent me, my brothers, and my sister off to school each morning well fed with lunches or lunch money and an expectation that we would do what we were supposed to do once we got there. I did anything but. I did not know it at the time, but I'd ended up the loser in the grand scheme of things. Eventually I finally settled down enough to think about school, and a career, and when I did, I find out that I had to go all the way back to ground zero, and that I did not get to pass go or collect $200.00 dollars. My "wake the fuck up" call was shocking.

I was in high school at the time the Black film movement was taking place. The term for it today is "Blaxploitation." It was a very exciting time for me, because I was a teenager, I was into popular Black culture, and those films addressed issues I knew well. The Black youth and young adults of my generation loved these films. All the hits were played and almost every month, there was a new film featuring our very finest actors of the day. We watched, Bill Cosby, Sidney Poitier, Harry Belafonte, Richard Pryor, Judy Pace, Sheila Fraser, Melvin Van Peebles, Pam Grier, Antonio Fargas, Calvin Lockhart, Redd Foxx, Godfrey Cambridge, James Earl Jones, Cleavon Little, Dick Anthony Williams, Ron O'Neal, Max Julien, Fred Williamson and others.

Pasadena had a local movie house, Cinema 21, and Sunday night-whoa Sunday night you could go to Cinema 21 to see and be seen. Everything was going on at the movies on a Sunday night, and everybody was there. It was the one place where you could see the city's Black folks between the ages of 14 and 50 in all their glory. The theater showed movies all day, of course, but you went to Cinema 21 Sunday evening's to be in the mix and to have something worthwhile to talk about Monday at school. I loved going to the movies on Sunday nights, but my parents were wise to the riff-raff there, and they rarely, if ever, wanted me in that company. They were very protective of my brothers and me and did all that they could to steer us away from the temptations lurking around young men coming of age.

I enrolled in City College after high school. I didn't really know what I was doing, and I figured it was the thing to do. I hadn't a plan for myself, so it was the easiest path to take. I knew I was going to have to do something. My parents were not going to let me sit around and do nothing. Further, for me to try and to explain to them why I wasn't interested in college was not going to go over well. I was aware that I hadn't done anything remotely promising while in high school. I wasn't fully aware of how behind I was until I took a trip to the college registrar's office to register.

That day there were two women manning the office. I casually strode in high school transcripts in hand, ready to enter college. After a brief introduction about why I was there, I produced my transcripts as requested. What happened next, I was not expecting. The first lady was looked at the transcripts and then looked up at me. She called the second woman over for a look-see. They both stood there looking as in disbelief, then laughed, and this was followed by more laugher. They could not believe I had the nerve or gumption to show up as if I were ready to go to school and compete. I guess they realized their lack of professionalism, and the laughter stopped. They took the time to address me and to explain what I'd need to do to enter school. I was going to have to take a bunch of remedial classes to make up for my dismal GPA. That day was literally a kick in the teeth.

After completing four years of high school, I knew little more than I did when I entered as a freshman. I thank God for my good genes, which were fortunately based on my DNA makeup from my mom, dad, grandparents, and so on going all the way back to Adam. I had enough organic knowledge to get by. But after high school graduation, with no more training wheels, I was going to have to learn and be accountable. Both were foreign to me. And so, I entered Pasadena City College (PCC). I began to crash and burn right away. Once again, the bad habits I had perfected were not going to allow me the opportunity to learn, be accountable, or any other thing productive. I was a professional slacker, and in that I had a PhD. I barely made it through my first semester, and it was obvious I could not do the school thing. I had been to a few parties during the fall of my first year, at PCC and I had run into a couple friends of mine who had gone to the military. I had no idea those guys had quietly disappeared, but they had, and I was finding out they were in the Army, Navy, and other branches, traveling and having a good time. I filed that away to think about later. One night, sometime later, I was smoking weed with Tony, and we began to talk about change in our lives.

Buddy Buddy System

Tony was a smart guy, and like me, I think he suffered from stunted growth due to the shenanigans that had become a part of our everyday lives. In our circle of friends, Tony was accepted as being smart and was often referred to as "the Professor." One-night, Tony and I, high as taxes (smoking), started talking about going into the military. For some strange reason, the conversation began to take on a serious tone, and we were really in the planning stages of making a move into the military. The next day, we picked up the conversation and really began strategizing how we'd go about enlisting. It was really happening. Tony and I found out we could enter the military together on something called the buddy-buddy plan, whereby friends enlisted together. We decided we would go into the Air Force. The next conversation, we picked a day and went to the local recruiter's office to begin talks with the Air-Force recruiter about joining. That branch was popular at that time, and we were told there was a wait period to enlist. Okay, cool-we had gotten ourselves worked up about this whole idea and wanted to execute the plan before we changed our minds. We went across the hall to speak with a guy from the Navy. The Navy was just as popular as the Air-Force, and it also had a wait period for enlisting. We ruled out the Marines, because we figured that in the event of some act of aggression, the Marines would be the first to respond, and although we were willing to serve our country, we weren't about fighting; we were mostly getting off the streets, making some paper, and going home. After we nixed the idea of the Marines, we went over to see the Army recruiter. The Army recruiter said, "Oh hell yeah; we'll take you right now." Tony and I said, "Whoa GI Joe, hold your horses; we're just talking for now."

The recruiter gave us the spill, top to bottom, on everything. Actually, he was very informative and took Tony and me out to lunch that day. We heard him out, and, after discussing what we'd heard amongst ourselves, we went back the next day and enlisted. We decided it was the thing to do. I knew I was not in the mood for school. I had not the ability to focus on school nor to study in a meaningful way. I needed a change of environment, and the military was offering me a fresh start. Tony felt the same way. We enlisted in the buddy – buddy plan, tested well and chose the option of joining an Army Security Agency.

I did not discuss my plan to join the military with my parents beforehand. I needed to do something for myself, and I needed to be the one to make the decision. I believe that for me, right at that precise time, I was beginning to experience some sliver of budding adulthood with a need to prove something, anything, to myself first and others second. Once my parents found out about the plan, they were supportive. They did, however have some disappointment, because they knew I had solid academic qualities that were going to waste. But enlisting gave me an additional kinship with my dad. He had been a military guy, and I knew he'd be able to relate to what my experience was going to be and could offer guidance. I was right, too, because we had some very significant conversations during my time in the military. He wrote to me and the letters were substantive and not just fluff. I appreciated hearing from him. A plus was that he knew where I was at all times, and I believe that was reassuring for him and my mom.

Sometime early in our induction into the Army, we underwent an interview process. In my interview, I admitted to smoking weed and not being casual about it, but chronic. I thought, "What the heck," a clean slate meant telling the truth, and what could they do? I had already enlisted. Well, they withdrew their ASA offer for me, but Tony kept quiet and remained in. It was all good, though. We went through basic training and AIT together, and then I left Fort Ord for Fort Stewart, Georgia and Tony remained nearby the Bay Area, on duty at the Presidio of San Francisco. I was not at Ft. Stewart very long, maybe a week, and then I was transferred north to Savannah, Georgia to a facility known as Hunter Army Airfield. It was a small base right in the middle of Savannah.

I was quite lucky in my military career; I fell into some sweet jobs and I found that I could do the military thing. I mean, I was good at soldiering. At Hunter, I had two primary jobs, one was as an administrative assistant and one was as a sedan driver for the base commander, Colonel Phillips. The colonel had two drivers: one who drove a Jeep, and me, who drove the sedan. Most of the time, when the colonel went anywhere on base, he did so by using his Jeep. But if he was on official business, he used the sedan which meant, I drove. Funny thing is both the other driver and I went by the name "Mac." The Jeep driver's last name was Mack and I, a McClain, was also called "Mac" for short.

Both Mack and I took pride of ownership in our positions and our cars. We washed and polished those vehicles as if they were our most cherished vehicles ever. I will admit that Mack did a much better job of caring for his Jeep than I did of the sedan. I took good care of the car, but Mack went to extraordinary lengths to keep that Jeep sparkling. He loved that Jeep and he loved the status of being seen with the Colonel. I did too. One assignment I had was to go to a helipad and pick up dignitaries. I took every opportunity to chat with whoever was there. Most of the time, it was a General visiting for one reason or another.

Another time, I was to drive the colonel and two other high-ranking officers to Fort Stewart for a meeting. The drive was almost a straight shot from Hunter down an interstate and then I took parallel road that took us directly into Fort Stewart. The second road was bordered by steep banks. At the bottom of the embankments was the beginning woods.

It was my first journey to the South as a young man alone. I was not used to seeing wild nature like I saw on those long drives back roads in the South. We started out about 10:00 a.m. with the aim to be at Stewart by about noon. Well, about an hour into the drive, I started getting sleepy. It was a hot, summer morning, muggy as heck, and I had eaten a heavy breakfast that morning. My body was trying to process the food and battle the heat and humidity all at the same time. I remember we had the air conditioner on, but it wasn't making a bit of difference with four of us in the car. I was driving and trying like a crazy person to stay awake, but every now and again, I felt myself nodding off. What was crazy was that I looked around the car and realized that everyone else was also asleep. It was as if the car was full of carbon monoxide and we were slowly being poisoned. I remember thinking, "If I don't get it together and stay awake, we're going to go right off the side of this road, down a ravine and into snake infested waters." I knew that to be the truth because one time, before I had driven the colonel to Stewart for a site visit, I parked the car in the same spot for a couple hours. When we returned to the car to leave, we saw five snakes resting in the shade beneath the car. It was trippy and scary to see those snakes all coiled up underneath the carriage of the car. I had a moment trying to unlock the door to get in and get out of there.

I did catch a second wind and found the strength to stay awake during the drive. Thank God, I did not kill us and no one in the car realized the amount of danger associated with that drive. Had the colonel had an inkling of what I was going through trying to stay awake, he would have been cussing at me the whole way. Normally, he was a gentle man, but he did have his military moments.

I made friends in Savannah and enjoyed my time there. Savannah was a small, beautiful, historic city in Georgia. It had weeping willow trees that lined the streets near the downtown area, and it had a Southern charm which it had been able to maintain for years. It was near a South Carolina state border, and we used to go over to South Carolina on some weekends to party. But I didn't have a good understanding of the South at the time; I mean, I had almost no understanding other than what I had been told about the South by my parents, but they had described the South as it was when they were growing up. I was there in 1976 more than 30 years later and I found myself learning everything on the fly.

A young lady in the military, stationed at the same base as I was, liked me and while I couldn't commit to a relationship because I had a girlfriend back at home, we did become fast friends, and we hung out together from time to time. She was Caucasian, which to me meant nothing, but in the South in 1976, it wasn't particularly cool to be seen in an interracial friendship. Even though Savannah was small relative to larger cities and was aware of its military base, interracial couples, i.e., black men and white women, were not normal. I was way out to lunch mentally on this, and my reality, which was growing up in California, was far from the reality Savannah. One night, one of the guys from the base had a party at his house which was out near Savannah State College, and my friend and I went. After the party, we were on our way back to the barracks, around 1:00 a.m. We stopped at a donut place; it might have been Krispy Kreme. There were three white guys in the place. I got out of the car, but left the car running so I could just quickly grab a few donuts. It wasn't until long after I was gone from the donut spot and safe back at the barracks that I realized the white dudes had been looking at me as if to say, "Nigga, do you realize where you are, the time of night it is, and the fact that you've got a white girl in the car with you and you look like you've smoked a whole bale of weed?" The answer to that is no, I didn't realize the jeopardy I'd put myself in; yes, I had been smoking weed most of the night, and yes, for the young lady in the car was white. Let's just say I escaped drama that night.

I left Georgia after a year and went to Dongducheon, South Korea. I was stationed with the 2nd Infantry Division; our motto "Second to none." We were far north and close to the demilitarized zone, known as the "DMZ." I arrived in December, and it was colder than any other place I'd been before. Additionally, the area stunk, as far as I was concerned. I called home on Christmas day that year, the temperature was -18F with a wind chill factor of another -7F. The only thing I wanted was for someone to ship over some sunshine from LA. I had never been in such a cold climate in my life, and it made me miserable. It was so cold frostbite was waiting around the corner if you did not protect your extremities, and generally your skin, from exposure. We had to do physical training drills every day at 6:00 a.m. The drills were a series of calisthenics followed by a five-mile run. In the winter, it was brutal, because it was so cold. There was only one way to get relief from the PT drills. There were no drills when the temperature was below -5F. Everyone in the barracks woke up on winter mornings, turned on the radio, and tuned in to the military weather channel to wait for the report for our city. The radio station went city by city listing the weather. There was immediate jubilation anytime we heard the weather was -4F or less. We celebrated like crazy, because it meant another hour of sleeping and no PT drills.

Korea was a different experience from anything I'd known. I felt a connectedness, or kinship to the location because my dad had been in Korea, only he had been there in the throes of war. I was there during a time of peace, but it proved to be challenging on a whole new level. I believe Korea was a time in my life during which I was forced to grow up. Looking back, I realize I had to make difficult personal decisions regarding my life. There were lots of things to do outside of working and soldiering, and not all of them were good. The place was a minefield of temptations. Any young man away from home, with disposable income, time on his hands, and a series of encouraged vices to partake in was going to find navigating those vices a daunting challenge.

I made a few good friends while there, but I also made a lot of bad decisions. I got involved in a money-making scam. I'm using the word "scam" loosely. It wasn't a bad deal, but doing what I did could have gotten me penalized by the military if I were found to be in violation of my orders. I was baited into it by someone who was my friend. In my totally naïve, trusting state, I fell for it and it was intended to make me look stupid to others and make it appear that I was susceptible to the enticement of money over loyalty and friendship. My brotha reputation took a huge hit, and friends distanced themselves from me because of the incident.

In the military, there are no secrets, so you know right away whether you're in or out with the people you surround yourself with. I was out, I recovered, but it took time and humility. I did learn from that lesson, but I went on to make a similar mistake later. What were not always apparent to me were the motives of those who'd come into my circle. I was usually willing to give the benefit of the doubt, as I was not looking to see if someone was morally corrupt or not, as judgement was not mine. I believed that as brothers, we were all about the same thing, but we were not. As for myself, dollars and cents had never been an underlying motivation for doing sinister things, but I had taken my eye off the ball, so of speak and I let others influence me in ways that were morally unhealthy. At any rate, Korea was a new and sometimes exciting experience.

Jimmy Carter was in office as president during my time in Korea. We had one serious incident that called for political diplomacy. The brigade I was in was near the DMZ, and we were put on standby alert in the event there would be a need for military action. Luckily, the situation was resolved through dialogue. Going to war was far from what I hoped to do in the military.

From Korea, I went to Fort Eustis, Virginia, where I stayed nine months. Fort Eustis was cool, but again, I was in the South and unaware of race relations. Being from California shielded me from the harsh realities of how race and people were perceived in the South. The details of specific interactions I had with white people off the base escape me, but suffice to say, once again, I drew the attention of a white female soldier who found herself attracted to me. We went out to a movie in Newport News. It was just my luck that Hampton Institute, a very popular historic Black college, was having movie night at the same theatre we were at. We received some less than welcome looks, and by the end of the night, welcomed the opportunity to get back to the safety of the base.

As my time in the military neared its end, I needed to decide what I was going to do. After giving it some thought, to exit the military, or re-enlist I decided to re-enlist for an additional three years. But when reenlisting I asked to go to Europe. One reason I did was because the first three years went quickly-so fast, in fact, that I hadn't noticed. I was doing okay for myself, making friends, working, and saving money, and I had not thought about what I would do if I got out of the military and went home. So, it made sense to continue on the journey and reenlist.

The assignment was Virginia, and it was excellent. The people I worked with and my officers wanted me to stay there. There was a promise of sending me to non-commissioned officers academy (NCO) if I stayed. I worked at an Army training post, and there were not more than five military personnel posted on my assignment. I was one half of two non-commissioned soldiers on the assignment and the other three were officers: one captain, one lieutenant colonel, and one brigadier general. The others in the office were general schedule (GS) workers. I wasn't familiar with the term "GS worker" initially, but I learned about GS rankings, and the work they did as a team.

One thing that got total office participation almost every time was killer tuna sandwiches we ordered about once a week from a local deli. The sandwiches were the most delicious tuna sandwiches I had ever eaten, and the kicker was that they put jalapeno peppers on them. They were mouthwatering, and everyone in the office would partook.

I recall the general being a really cool guy. He was mild mannered and very easy to talk too. There was also one other Black guy in the office. He was a high-ranking non-commissioned officer, a master sergeant, very good at his job, and well liked, with an easy personality, and he was kind of mentor to me. He chatted me up about a variety of things all the time, and he encouraged me in many ways; and he was the most vocal person asking me to stay in my current job. I appreciated his confidence in me.

At the time I was in Virginia, my girlfriend's brother was in the Marines at Camp Lejeune in North Carolina, not far away. We wrote back and forth to each other a few times, and I always appreciated hearing from him. He was a captain at the time, and he, too, encouraged me and pushed for me to get back into school, or, if I was going to stay in the military, to do so on the commission side. But I wanted to travel, and so I left Virginia and went to Germany, which was a wild ride. I spent three years there before deciding to end my active duty.

Horace Grayling Thompson was my roommate for a time there. He and I were fast friends, and then best friends, and he remains one of my best and closest friends to this day. We exited the military months apart, and I venture to say that for the first 10 years we were out of the military, we spoke on the phone at least one a month, usually more. We were the poster children for the AT&T campaign-"Reach out and touch"; this was at the same time as cell phones.

Finding Life

I got married for the first time in 1983. My first wife, Cindie and I had been dating for years, and our marriage was a natural progression. We both wanted to be married, and married to each other, so we thought, "Why not?" We settled into married life and it really was no different than when we were dating. Cindie was smart, funny, outgoing, and fiercely loyal, although she could also be overbearing on occasion; this is just my opinion. By any standard, she was a good if not great wife. My father-in-law was very nice to me, but never had a lot to say. He was a very quiet man, completely introspective and introverted. He delighted in cooking Sunday dinners for us, and we delighted in eating the meals he prepared. He was also excellent with his hands and mechanically inclined, so we saved a lot of money on plumbing bills and knick knack things that I could not do around the house or make myself. My father-in-law was more than willing to do things if we asked.

Cindie's mother passed away while I was in the Army. I felt bad that I was not home at that time, and Cindie did not tell me right away. I learned of her passing through my parents. I was not there to console her at a time when I am sure she needed me most. I cannot imagine the pain and despair she had to process on her own. Cindie had an older brother, an aunt, cousins, and friends who all pitched in to help, but I wasn't there, and I know that if I had suffered the same type of loss, she would have wanted to be there for me. Cindie remained mostly quiet about her mother's passing.

I believe that thinking about it made it worse, and she chose to move beyond it. She was strong in that way-quietly resolute.

Cindie and I became parents four years our marriage. My daughter, Stephanie, was loved from conception, and is in many ways, equal parts her mother and me. I believe Cindie wanted kids right from the beginning. We got married in our late 20s and many of my wife's friends had already had children. I don't recall really giving it much thought initially but I imagined it was in the plans somewhere down the road. We had conversations here and there about having children, but again, I imagined the children would come when they came. At some point, maybe two to three years into our marriage we began to try purposely to have a child. We weren't always successful in our attempts. I hadn't realized that the science behind getting pregnant could be challenging.

My wife was pregnant one time prior to carrying Stephanie to term. The first pregnancy ended with a miscarriage. We were disappointed, and for a very brief time, thought the possibility of having a child might be lost. But soon after, she conceived again, and that time the pregnancy held. My wife was a nurse and knew to do the clinical stuff she was supposed to do. There was the pre-natal care, watching what she ate, and exercising regularly, while I did the companion stuff, such as running to the store for the funny food cravings, never speaking about weight gain, and that sort of thing. I was very excited and onboard with becoming a father. We even went through Lamaze classes. I recall us going to class on the day a birthing video was shown. It was one of the most disturbing movies I had ever witnessed. To be fair, the real thing is nothing like the movie. During the movie, I passed out. Man, the video was in color and everything was larger than life on the screen. I felt myself becoming nauseous early on, and then I began to sweat and squirm in place. I thought, "Oh no, this here is way too real," but I couldn't leave the class, and I didn't want to seem squeamish in front of everyone. So, I sat there like an idiot and collapsed on the floor as the baby was born. I needed serious attention after the film. I was so messed up. My breathing was labored, I was sweating, I felt completely ill, and all the while, I thought, "This is just a film; I'm going to have to witness this live and in color sometime in the next two months." I did witness my daughter's birth, however, and it was a beautiful moment. My wife was a real trooper.

Stephanie's birth was especially beautiful because we had suffered the miscarriage earlier. Cindie was very careful carrying Stephanie, so when she got into her third trimester and we were sure she would be okay, we were elated. But we had another miscarriage after Stephanie, which was heartbreaking for us. There are many things said about bringing a child into the world, and you hear these things at different times during your child's growth and development, such as "They don't come with a manual," "Every child is born with its own blessing," and "No child gets out of childhood without suffering some injury." The third saying is what got us.

Cindie returned to work at the children's hospital right around the time Stephanie was one. She opted for the 3:00 p.m. to 11:00 p.m. shifts the weekdays, but on the weekends, she worked 7:00 a.m. to 5:00 p.m. shifts. Cindie and I quickly learned our daughter's habits. By the time Stephanie was 18 months old and walking, we had baby proofed the house as much as we could. There were just the three of us, and we gave Stephanie plenty of attention. But at that time tragedy struck. Cindie had to work on a Saturday the accident happened. She woke up early around 5:30 a.m., had breakfast, set out food for me to feed Stephanie, got herself ready for work, and left the house. Stephanie was awake, which meant I had to get up. So, I got out of bed, got breakfast for Stephanie and for myself, and proceeded to clean the kitchen. Stephanie had been awake for about four hours and I knew she'd be ready for bed in about another hour. I washed the dishes done and put on a small pot of water to boil for tea. We did not have a teapot at the time, so I boiled water in a small cooking pot. When it came to a full boil, I poured myself a cup of tea and took it over to our dining room table. About the time I placed the tea on the table, I noticed Stephanie had a dustpan in her hand. I went to take it away from her, because she was at the age when she put everything in her mouth. When I went over to grab the dustpan, she ran behind me and within 10 seconds, she was screaming and my tea cup was on the floor and shattered. Initially, I did not comprehend what had happened and I could see her t-shirt was soaked in the front and steam was coming off it. I grabbed her as quickly as possible. My mind was racing on what to do. I could see Stephanie looking at me, puzzled and wondering what the heck was going on, and then her focus shifted to what she was feeling and she started screaming again.

I made an awful mistake that I did not realize would be a mistake at that moment, and I lifted her shirt. When I did, the skin on her chest peeled away from her body. "Oh my God! What do I do?" I thought. I panicked, it seemed like eternity, but it was only seconds later that I dialed 9-1-1. I will always remember the fire unit that came to my house. It was from the station not far from our house. They were at our house in no time flat. The truck arrived, and a fire fighter jumped off the truck, burst through my front door, grabbed Stephanie out of my arms, ran to the kitchen sink, and started dousing her with cold water. He ran her tiny little body under it repeatedly, all while talking with her, and reassuring her. Others radioed the hospital to have things in place for our arrival. The fire fighter's actions were coordinated and done with immediate precision. The fire truck's siren and associated activity brought all my neighbors out to see what the commotion was. Mrs. Johnson, my neighbor, rushed over to see if there was anything she could do, but at that time, there wasn't. She cried, and said, "No, not the baby, not the baby." Nobody knew what was going on, but they were all concerned and upset.

When I needed to leave with the ambulance, I did not have to say anything to my neighbors. I knew everyone, and they knew us. They were going to take care of my house, and that was understood. As I mentioned earlier, we lived in a beautiful neighborhood in Northwest Pasadena, about a mile from the Rose Bowl. Everyone knew everyone else. It was the type of neighborhood where everyone had manicured lawns, and yards with fences and we spoke to each other. I rode in the ambulance with Stephanie to the hospital, and my neighbors closed my house for me.

I tried with no luck to reach Cindie at work. I must have a called a dozen times, but there was no answer. I called my parent's house and asked them to come to the hospital. They asked me over the phone to explain why, but I did not. My voice was broken, and I had been crying. They knew it had to be Stephanie, and my dad would not come. He did not want to process anything harmful happening to Stephanie. But my mother and my sister come, for that difficult time.

The hospital staff went to work on Stephanie, immediately, providing the necessary medical attention to treat her. She had second and third degree burns on over 30% of her upper body. I learned later that a child's skin at that age is paper thin. While the hot water would have been just hot to me, and likely wouldn't have scalded me, it was nearly life threatening to my daughter.

While I was in the room with Stephanie and the nurses were treating her, I was approached by a very non-threatening and non-assuming young white man. He introduced himself and begin to ask me questions. I was shaken up, but I answered them. Then I noticed him looking at the nurses, and they were looking back at him; there was some kind of communication going on. I don't know how I picked up on it, but I did. I realized that the young man was a social worker and his questions were to determine whether my daughter's injuries were the result of an accident or were done to her on purpose. I was very upset that they thought I could have done something like that on purpose to my daughter. Cindie worked at Children's Hospital, and she had horror stories of children being brought in with injuries consistent with abuse. Those incidents made her sick. I remembered this, and reasoned the young man had a job to do and part of that job was to ask me those questions.

Initially, my daughter was at the hospital in town, but once they stabilized her, they put us in an ambulance and transferred her to our preferred hospital, which was not far away. My mother and sister followed. At that point 5:00 p.m. was approaching and I still had not been able to reach Cindie, but I knew she would be home soon and I did not want her to hear about the accident from neighbors, I asked my mother to take me home.

When I got home, the neighbors began to ask me questions about Stephanie's condition. I told them she was stabilized and that I had not been able to reach Cindie all day. We were all outside when she arrived from work. She pulled her car into the driveway, waved hello to everyone, and went directly inside the house. I left everyone outside and went in. She asked me where Stephanie was, and I recounted the accident to her. At first, she thought it was some sort of joke in bad taste. After the realization that what I was saying had indeed occurred, she wanted to leave immediately for the hospital. We got there, and the hospital staff directed us to Stephanie's room. She was asleep. We stayed together for about two hours, and Cindie said she was going to stay the night. I stayed a bit longer, and then I drove home.

Stephanie was released from the hospital after another day and began recovering at home. The worst part of the recovery for her was having to take baths. They required us to take off the old bandages, wash the burned area of her body to remove any dead skin, dry the area, apply ointment, and rewrap her body. Stephanie knew the routine and would begin crying and as soon as she heard the bath water running. It was painful for her mother and me, too.

I believe we all cried during some of those baths. Eventually, the sessions got better. Stephanie got stronger, and the healing process rapidly picked up.

One evening, long after Stephanie had recovered, she and I were at my parents' house during one of our routine trips at the end of the day. Stephanie was playing around, and my dad asked her what happened to her-and why she was wearing the bandages on her body. Stephanie said, "My dad burned me." I was horrified, while Stephanie just laughed. She doesn't remember much about her grandfather. There are pictures of him, and pictures of the two of them together, but she does not remember the joy she brought to him.

Autumn

In the late 80s homes in California, and in Southern California, in particular appreciated yearly at a phenomenal rate. Our neighborhood enjoyed robust returns on home appreciation. Cindie was back at work after having a child, and I had moved from one company to another. We found ourselves in healthy financial condition. It was at this time that we decided to do a remodeling project. We went room by room, determining what we would do. We selected the various contractors we'd use for the project, and when we finalized our plans, we got the project underway. We painted, put in new windows, doors, and floors, landscaped our front and back yards, removed trees, gutted and restored our kitchen, upgraded our bathrooms, the whole nine yards. One part of the remodel was the removal of an avocado tree.

Cindie and I had a huge Hass avocado tree in our yard. The tree produced hundreds of avocados. They were thick-skinned and meaty inside. During avocado season, they were abundant. Cindie bagged them up in big brown shopping bags and gave them away to the neighbors. She walked the neighborhood and left a bag of avocadoes at the front door of each house. At a nearby market called (Chan's), she was also able to sell some of the avocadoes. We couldn't do anything with hundreds of avocadoes so this is how we gave them away, so they wouldn't go rotten. We eventually pulled the tree up, because the roots of the tree began to damage our driveway and tear away at our lawn.

The renovation project took months but we finally finished in the early spring of 1990. The remodel was a success, and we had neighbors over all the time to see the finished work. One bonus for a certain contractor who worked on our project was that he was asked to do two jobs for two different neighbors once our project was completed.

Almost, immediately after the remodel we put the house on the market. With the upgrades and the location, we could ask for top dollar on the house. The sale was contingent on whether we found a new place. We house hunted for about a month before we received a call about a house that was going on the market in a matter of days. We were given a first look at the house by our realtor. I saw it first, and once I did, I knew Cindie would love it. She saw it, and yep, she loved it. Prior to seeing the house, we received and negotiated the sale of our home. Once the deal was put into motion, it was not more than a month later that everything came together. We sold our home in Pasadena, and bought a new home in Altadena. Both sales and the move happened during the first week of October 1990. Within a week of the sale, Cindie threw a princess themed birthday bash for Stephanie at the new house to celebrate her third birthday. My parents were very proud of our purchase of the new house. It signified hard work and a real come up. But two weeks after we'd moved in, in the early morning of October 25th, 1990, I received a phone call, that was followed by a chain of events that changed the course of my life.

Just as a father knows his son, a son knows his father. My dad, although not perfect, was far better at living and conducting himself than I was. The standard I use to analyze our lives (his and mine) is a moral coding that is innately me. It is as much a part of me and my DNA makeup. It is that knowledge that courses through me and feeds me.

Who are we, and what are we, if we do not learn from within and live using that education? My father is an example of someone who lived according to self-knowledge and trusting what he knew to be the path of his life. I could say any number of things to explain the differences between me and my dad, but the raw truth is that, he was the better man. I say that not with envy or jealousy; I say it simply looking into the rear-view mirror of my life. How much did I waste on people, places, and things that got me nowhere or gave me nothing in return? My mother hates for me to say this, but I always tell her God is going to give us a do-over. This life is just a test to prepare you for what lies ahead. I don't know if that is true or not, but I put it out there so often in the universe that it almost seems real now. Stay tuned.

The love I feel and have for my children is as strong as any love I've ever known. I fell in love with each of them at conception, and that love has only grown stronger throughout their lives. I cannot imagine my life without them, and I am certain they were written into my life plan from the beginning. They are, as individuals, completely different from each other in spirit, character, and behavior, but they have a very strong bond. They all carry, for good or bad, the McClain look. A very strong and prominent facial recognition has been assigned to the McClain's. It is easy to see the McClain in my children, as some say. I am different from my father in that I hug, kiss, and continuously tell my children I love them. I can't help it, and I consider my role as their father a blessing.

I attended the birth of each child, and with each birth, I was moved to tears. The process of conception to birth has deepened my constitution and ability to do all that I can to help my children grow into their very best selves. I use humor, cajole them, encourage them, and discipline them, so that they see and know that nothing worth having is out of their reach. The world seems so different now than when I was a kid, teenager, and young adult. The minefield for kids today is everywhere, and any deviation from a total focus on what society deems valuable can have your family physician prescribing Ritalin and insisting ADHD is the problem.

My job has taken me out of the country and away from my children for months at a time. I miss them terribly when I'm gone, and I know they miss me. My parenting style has been to mix being their father with befriending them. I liken it to being a "dad and dude" cocktail. I try to listen to my kids. I try to hear every word said, and I try to imagine what they're not telling me. I try to remember how I pushed boundaries with my parents, and focus on the moments I have with my children. I stress that an honorable conversation is one in which both my children and I are honest. My kids have reached age at which they are too advanced for some punishments. I try the best I can to help my kids understand their choices and the consequences of their decisions. I am one of millions of parents trying to steer my children on the right path. I care that my children are educated, physically well, and socially accepted.

It has been stated that all time is relative and that each generation has its own challenges. It has also been stated that there isn't anything more stressful now than what was faced by earlier generations nor things be more stressful for generations come. Growing up, I did have pressures, but I did not have to deal with cyberbullying, or mass shootings in schools, movie theaters, concert halls, and restaurants. I was not subjected to teenage suicide, opioid addiction, and the sex slave trade. Children today, millennials and younger, have come into a far different world than the one that existed when I was a teenager.

I have hope in America. I've seen the best of our country, and I've seen some things that are forgettable. I'm hoping for an American experience for my children in which the hue of their skin makes no difference in public or private. An experience in which opportunity exists for my daughters as well as my sons. I'm hoping the Obama presidency wasn't a one-off. The U.S. is ready to see a second, third, fourth, and later president who represents the diversity of the country.

Being away from home for long stretches of time is difficult. The economy and the type of work I do dictates it, and it is simply how things are at this time. Separation from family and all that I love challenges me daily. I miss holidays, birthdays, and a host of other gatherings people would like me to attend. My family is repeatedly asked the same question: "When is Kenny coming home." It's exhausting for them and makes them relive my absence. My family is very generous in their ability to be supportive of me as it's how my work is, but being without me at home is a sacrifice.

I meditate and pray, and although I pray more than I meditate, and there's a difference between the two. I believe in the healing properties attached to using the head, heart, and soul. I think about my mortality as I am entering my senior years and beginning to experience the loss of older loved ones and peers. I have joked in the past with close friends and made a promise. It is as follows: if one or all of my friends gets a call that I have passed away, I need them to speak at my funeral. I do not want a generic eulogy. I want personal references made by friends and family. I have sworn to do the same in the event I get a call that someone I know personally has passed away. I was asked quite unexpectedly to speak at the funeral of a longtime friend and neighbor. The family decided to ask three people-representing, work, family, and community. I spoke for the community in which he lived. I was terrified at the outset, because I had no experience speaking in public. Further, I was going to be a representative of him and his family with the words I chose to speak. However, I did do it, and all was well. What I got from the experience, I believe, was a sense that I was able to add a personal feel to who he was, and how he lived-as I knew him. I believe his family and others at the funeral appreciated the words I spoke. I want personal words spoken about me by those who know me best.

A direct result of my job and my travel is that I am now friends with people all over the world. I have been to homes, had meals, and attended cultural rituals that are new to me. Once upon a time, I would not have been able to foresee these things occurring in my life. I never take these blessings for granted and receive them with eyes wide open. I appreciate the fullness with which I am able to live.

I wish my Dad were around today. I have traveled the world, and seen some things, that we could discuss. He would be proud of me. This I know.

Epilogue

My dad had a habit of visiting his sisters on Sundays after church. Sometimes, we would all go and sometimes, my dad would drop us at home and double back for a visit. He was consistent in this routine. My uncle George, who was married to my dad's oldest sister, had a knack for giving nicknames. He was very fond of my dad, and my dad was equally fond of him. Uncle George deemed my dad "the Deacon" because of his steadfastness in attending church every Sunday. The name stuck.

As I got older and went my own way, I did my part to visit family without prompting from my mom and dad. On occasion, I stopped by my aunt Myrlean and uncle George's house to visit and talk about any and everything. My aunt and uncle loved my company, and I was always welcome there. I also knew, there would be something delicious to eat, as my aunt was a great cook and there was always plenty of food in the house. Southern hospitality runs deep in my family, and we can't visit anyone's house without them offering a plate of food. So, I would go by there after work some days and just visit. My uncle always encouraged me no matter the topic. He was keenly interested in my personal growth in the job. He always asked if I was learning, if I liked my job, and what my long-term plans and goals were. I always discussed the various engineering projects I was working on and the role I played in those projects. He was consistent in this reminder: in all that you do, do your best; honest evaluations require commitment in uncovering ugly truths, and to thine own self, be true.

My uncle was also a capitalist, and as such, he said, "There is no shame in asking for pay equal to my contribution." He called it "dropping iron." He was funny that way. One evening, I stopped by their house after work to tell my uncle I had gotten a raise and a promotion at work. On the spot, he deemed me "the Wheel."

The nickname is a reference to someone who is a big deal, as in the Big Wheel. The name stuck.

Acknowledgements

To my mother, I love you. You have been a rock and pillar for me since the beginning. Being your first born has been extremely rewarding.

To my sister Valerie, I never knew I could love a sibling as much as I love you. You are Chaka Khan's every woman. I cannot put into words how much I love and appreciate you. Being your big brother is a journey filled with joy day to day.

To my brothers Myron Keith, Gregory, and Gerald (RIP), I love you. I've got your back. If there is a second go-around in life, I'll sign up to be your brother again, providing you let me.

To Stephanie, (Boo) Kennedy, (Boo) and Josh (Nasir), – who knew parenting would be so overly rewarding. I had to have you in my life. I have come to know that you were written into my plan since the beginning, and I would not have it any other way.

To Charles and Ellis, it is with joy that I live as your uncle. You make me so proud. I love you both, and I will forever be here for you.

To Gabby, you are my daughter, and I love you. I might have set your bar too high, but I believe in you. You have the goods, Gabby; make the world support your vision.

To my family and friends – you know who you are. You make my orbit complete. Without you, there is no me. I love you and appreciate your place in my life. Let's keep it going.